The Case of the Missing Macon County Men

Joe Grimsley

PublishAmerica
Baltimore

Softcover 9781462651993
PUBLISHED BY PUBLISHAMERICA, LLLP
www.publishamerica.com
Baltimore

Printed in the United States of America

The Case of the Missing Macon County Men

Joe Grimsley

Dedication

This book is dedicated to the memories of Larry Eugene "Mickey" Jones, Kenneth Lee "Kenny" Summers, and Larry Gene "Larry" Jones. Their foolish actions put them in the wrong place and a bad situation. They shouldn't have been where they were, but the results far outweighed the deserved punishment. They paid for their foolish actions with their lives, in a gruesome manner. I can only hope that where they are now, they are aware of the effort, dedication, and work involved in producing this book. May all of everyone's efforts be pleasing to them. Here's to you, guys!

May you now rest in peace!

The families of the victims shown above want to express a special recognition of gratitude to Carl Shoopman, whose help at a troubled time was above value. Words can not express our gratitude properly, so we say to Carl simply, thank you!

Chapter 1

September 3, 1985

The sun rose blood red that morning over the farm of Jerry Ward in Trousdale County, Tennessee, near the Kentucky border. As on other farms in the county, in September, the corn stalks on the Ward farm were a man's height, and there was a thicket of weeds equally high. Before the day ended, a hail of bullets would clip the leaves of the corn and weeds, and blood would stain the earth, and the state would be stunned by the terrible thing that happened there.

This is the low plateau of Tennessee, a broad area in the middle of the state, between the mountains to the east and the Tennessee River bottom to the west. It is slightly rolling terrain punctuated by small hills known as knobs and dotted with locust, sycamore, poplar, spruce, and maple trees. Tobacco is the main crop here, with corn and hay also growing in the fields of small farms. It is Protestant COUI).- try, Southern Baptist mostly, the heart of the Bible Belt, still largely a rural section of America, an area of family owned farms and small towns. The values of the average person are fundamentalist America-work, duty, God and Country, honesty. It is the home of country western music U.S.A. The folk style and speech reflect lingering traces of a less complicated, rural America.

From mid-afternoon on of that September 3, Jerry Ward's every action would later be a matter for minute public scrutiny and analysis. But at dawn that day, he stood in the doorway of his mobile home, looking toward the long rows of chicken coops that held dozens of expensive fighting gamecocks. Inside the mobile home, his young, pretty wife, Melinda, was sleeping, unaware of the role she would play in the deadly drama that would unfold before the sun went down that day.

Within sight of Jerry Ward's mobile home was the farmhouse where his mother, Grace Ward, lived, but she was not home that day.

Jerry Ward gazed anxiously in the direction of the barn and the thicket of weeds nearby that screened a crop thousands of times more valuable than corn or tobacco.

Jerry Ward had lived in the area all of his thirty years. During his school career at Trousdale County High in Hartsville, Jerry had been a local football hero. His hard-hitting prowess earned him an athletic scholarship to the University of Louisville. He had the build of a football running back, heavy, but all bulging muscle, without an ounce of fat. He stood six feet tall. His features were dark, his hair thick and curly, and he wore a mustache.

The Ward farm was located on farm-to-market road 141, a few miles south and across the river from Hartsville, a community of less than 2,000 persons.

Hartsville is a quiet southern town with dusty streets and frame buildings clustered around a two-story brick courthouse dating back to 1906. An hour's drive to the north lies the Kentucky border. An hour's drive to the southwest would suddenly take one out of the rural backwaters of small farms and isolated towns into the city of Nashville; Tennessee. That glittering country music capital of the world seems a continent away from downtown Hartsville, where numerous empty storefronts reflect a degree of economic stagnation. Typical of a small southern town, there is a Baptist church and a downtown cafe that is a social gathering place where hangs a Confederate flag beside a Lion's Club banner. In the 1970s, the Tennessee utility company began construction of a nuclear power plant a few miles outside Hartsville. The construction work had brought a temporary economic boom to the small community. In the panic following the Five-Mile nuclear disaster, however, the reactor project near Hartsville had been abandoned, construction workers moved away, and the town had faded back into a sleepy, isolated village with an insular attitude toward the outside world.

It is a town where neighbors know one another and a stranger is immediately noticed and treated with suspicion. Many who live here are distantly related, tracing their ancestors back to the original settlers. Among them are the Ward family, well known in the community. The first white child born in Trousdale County back in the 1700s was a Ward. The land owned by the original Ward settlers has been handed down to the present generation. It would be hard to find anyone in Trousdale County who didn't know first- or second-hand the Wards.

Jerry Ward lived across the river, south of Hartsville, on a section of Ward land. The farm property had on it a large barn, the farmhouse where Jerry's mother, Gracie Ward, lived, and the mobile home where Jerry lived with his twenty-two year old wife, Melinda. Across the road from the farmhouses was a large metal storage shed. On Jerry Ward's farm property was dozens of chicken coops. The coops housed hundreds of fighting gamecocks. The sport of fighting gamecocks has been outlawed, but it is not illegal to raise the cocks. Whether Jerry Ward only raised and sold the fighting roosters or was actively involved in the underground sport was a matter of speculation.

Later, there would be those who said Jerry Ward was a peaceful man who didn't cause trouble. Others would say that he was a professional gambler and that he was peaceful as long as you stayed on your side of the river and away from his property.

There was a reason Jerry Ward didn't want people nosing around on his property, a reason that might have caused him to give some anxious looks toward the thicket of weeds growing near the barn. There was a faint smell of skunk in the air. It came from a weed some called skunk weed because of the smell it gave off. It is a weed better known as marijuana.

That fall of 1985, there were patches of marijuana being cultivated in quite a few places in Trousdale County. The marijuana growing in the vicinity of Jerry Ward's barn, screened from view by high weeds and a wall-like fence, was a very high grade that local experts on the subject of marijuana called sinsemilla. It was cultivated by pulling up the male weed, isolating the female stalks, then harvesting the female buds. The crop on Jerry Ward's farm was about ready for harvesting.

Jerry Ward did not own the farm or the mobile home in which he lived. The farm property was owned by Jerry's mother, Grace. She acquired it in a divorce settlement with Jerry's father, Hubert Ward Jr. The mobile home Jerry lived in was owned by his brother Bobby, who also owned construction material in the metal storage building located across the road from the Ward buildings and mobile home. Bobby wielded the economic power behind the scenes in the Ward family. Bobby was the co-owner of the Reinhart and Ward Construction Company that employed Hubert Ward Jr., father of Jerry and Bobby.

As the clock ticked toward four p.m. of that fateful day, The principal players in the drama were converging on the Ward farm like puppets on a string, unable to escape their Horrible destiny.

That morning, a one-ton flatbed truck pulling a heavy-duty utility trailer pulled out of a Ward construction site in

Centerville, Tennessee, and headed for the metal storage building on the Ward farm to pick up pipe fittings and supplies. It was a several hours' drive. Driving the truck was forty-two year old Howard Collins, a construction worker employed by the Reinhart and Ward Company. Riding beside him was Jerry Ward's father, Hubert Ward Jr.

North of Hartsville, in adjoining Macon County, about a twenty minute drive from the Ward farm is Lafayette, Tennessee. That September day, Larry Gene Jones, age thirty-eight, was rambling around town in his four-wheel drive pickup truck with the radio tuned to a station that played country western music. He liked the basic country music-Johnny Cash, Loretta Lynn, Conway Twitty.

Larry had been hitting the bottle pretty hard for several hours. He was feeling no pain. Excitement was building in him. He was tinkering with a plan in his mind, something that was going to be both fun and an adventure, and profitable. The more he thought about it, the more impatient he became for school to let out. He wanted to take his son Mickey along. Mickey was in the junior class at Macon County High.

A week earlier, Larry Gene had driven his yellow Chevrolet pickup truck down highway 141 south of Hartsville. With him was a friend of Mickey's, twenty-year old Curt Fishburn. Larry Gene wanted to check out the marijuana patch on the Ward property.

Near the Ward farm, they had parked on the side of the road. They crawled over a fence, skirted a pond, went though a wooded area, and crept through the tall weeds toward the Ward barn. There was a cornfield behind the barn. At that point, Curt stopped. Larry Gene moved closer to the tall board fence that surrounded the area beside the barn where the marijuana was being cultivated. They could see the tops of the marijuana just above the fence. The peculiar smell of skunk given off by the weed wafted through the hot August air.

Suddenly, they heard the angry voice of Melinda Ward call out from somewhere on the other side of the barn. "You get off my property!"

Larry Gene didn't move.

"Get off my property," she repeated, "or I'll call the law.".

Larry Gene grinned. "What are you going to tell them that I'm stealing your marijuana?" he taunted. The stillness of the hot August day was shattered by a shotgun blast.

Melinda had fired into the air. Curt didn't wait around for a second shot. He took off running, crashing through the corn and high weeds. Larry Gene was close behind him, laughing. Ever since that day, a plan had been forming in Larry Gene's mind.

If the plan was reckless and dangerous, Larry Gene didn't bother to think about that. He tended to do things on impulse and worry about the cost later. He'd been living that way all his life. The fact that it had landed him in jail more than once didn't change his thinking pattern.

Larry Gene Jones was a Huckleberry Finn who never quite got the hang of the responsibility of adult life. It was his childlike, impulsive, generous nature that endeared him to all his relatives but was a pain in the neck to the authorities. By the time he was seventeen, his petty thefts had landed him in the penitentiary.

Individuals like Larry Gene Jones can be extremely charming. His first wife Sherry found him so when they met. She was a teenager when Larry swept her off her feet. He neglected to mention that he was on parole at the time.

This is how Sherry described him. "He was a likable person. You couldn't help but like him. He would give you the shirt offs his back, but then he would steal your shoes. That's just the way he was. He couldn't handle alcohol. A few drinks and he was liable to drive right down the middle of the road."

It was a stormy seven-year marriage. Sherry said, "Me and him would fight like cats and dogs. He went with everybody that had a skirt on. He wouldn't stay out of jail. He wouldn't hold down a job. He didn't support us. I couldn't keep him out of the house with his grandparents. If we got out on our own for a little while, he would quit his job and we would have to move back with his relatives. Larry was a strange person. He would tell you he was going to work, and he would call you after a while to let you know he was in jail.

"I put up with it for almost seven years, and then I had to go. I said if we stayed married, sooner or later, one of us would wind up killing the other one."

Sherry went on to a happy secure second marriage to Joe Grimsley. They had one daughter, Marsha. Larry Gene also remarried.

Sherry, however , remained close to Larry Gene's family and remained friends with Larry Gene.

She said, ''When I divorced Larry, I didn't divorce the rest of his family. I could go to them right now and tell them I needed a place to stay and I could stay at any of their houses. And, you know, it's really strange. After the divorce, Larry and I became real good friends even though I married someone else and so did he. After he remarried, I took his wife Shirley to the hospital the day their first child was born. Larry, as usual, was being completely irresponsible. He got to my house on a flat tire, and he was wearing ragged cut-offs and flip-flops. I drove his wife to ˙ the hospital, got her admitted, then came back and found some decent clothes for Larry. I took him to the hospital. I went to the grocery store, then back to the hospital and stayed with Larry until the baby came and we knew Shirley and the baby were all right. After the baby was born, I brought Larry back over to my house, fed him supper, and called his mother to tell his family the baby was born. Then I took him back to the hospital and I came home and went to bed. I was give out. But I would do anything I could for Larry and he would me, too. We made better friends than we did married people."

During their seven-year marriage, Sherry and Larry Gene had two boys, Larry Eugene Jones (he was nicknamed "Mickey") and Timmy. After the divorce and remarriage, Sherry lived with her second husband Joe Grimsley in Glasgow, Kentucky, near the Tennessee border. The younger boy, Timmy, lived with them. Mickey often visited the Grimsley home but spent most of his teenage years living with his grandmother, Inez Thaxton, in Lafayette, just across the border in Tennessee. Inez Thaxton was the mother of Mickey's father and Mickey's aunt, Pauline Summers, whom Mickey called "Aunt Polly." One of the Summers children was Kenny, Mickey's first cousin.

In spite of his irresponsibility and trouble with the law, Larry Gene was loved by his family. His generous nature made him a Santa Claus uncle. He was a soft touch, a constant source of candy and gifts to the kids in the family. Mickey's younger brother Timmy said, "Daddy was Mickey's idol. Mickey idolized Daddy."

When he had a job, Larry Gene worked mostly in construction either as a carpenter or mason's helper. He had basic skills in carpentry, but nothing to brag about. He did some factory work also. Over the years, he worked in a doughnut factory, boot factory, blouse factory, and furniture factory. In his pocket that day were two books of cigarette rolling papers, a wallet containing five photographs of his children and other relatives, a Tennessee driver's license that expired 1-17-89, a scrap of paper with "77 Chevy 4x4" written on it (the make and model of the truck he was driving), a Union local 2338 carpenters' card and $98.00 in cash. He was dressed in a dark blue button-down shirt and faded blue jeans.

During his lifetime, Larry Gene had collected a gallery of tattoos. On his right shoulder were letters spelling the name "Mickey." Also on his right shoulder was the tattoo of a dove. On his left breast was a tattoo of a woman, and on his left shoulder, the name "Timmy." An Indian chief decorated his left upper arm and a woman his lower left arm. Flower tattoos were on the back of his left hand. On the upper portion of the back of his right forearm were the words, "I Love You," and on the back of his right hand was a tattoo of a cross with the name "Billie" inside the cross. That afternoon of September 3, Larry Gene again looked impatiently at his watch, then turned his truck in the direction of his mother's home. Larry was ready for action. For the past four years, Mickey had been living with his grandmother, Inez Thaxton. He should be getting home any time now. School was over for the day.

Mickey didn't go straight home from school that day. When school let out, Mickey spent a half hour riding around with two friends. He arrived home at four o'clock. His grandmother said, "Your daddy has been by here looking for you."

"Did he say what he wanted?"

"No. I guess he'll be back, though. He was actin' like he wanted to find you real bad. I don't know what he's up to. Looked to me like he's been drinkin' pretty good."

"Well, tell him I'm going over to the Village Market for cigarettes. "

Mickey walked the short distance to the market where he

bought cigarettes and had a cold drink. When he returned, his grandmother said, "Your daddy came by again and I told him you was at the Village Market. Did he find you?"

"No. Guess we missed each other." "You want to go look for him?"

"I'll just set and wait. He'll come back here, I guess, if it's important."

Mickey was feeling good that day. It was great to be seventeen, healthy, with his life spread out ahead of him. He had lots of friends at school, was well-liked, and he had a job with CETA, a government program, that kept a little money in his pocket. To earn his CETA check, Mickey painted rooms at his school. Mickey was in the eleventh grade at Macon County High School in Lafayette. He was also taking some tenth grade classes to make up passing grades he'd missed the year before. In his wallet was a Tennessee State Proficiency Test # 5, indicating a passing score of 71.Mickey and his grandmother had to watch their money carefully. There were small Social Security disability checks that came in every month for his granny. Mickey added a share of his CETA checks to his grandmother's disability checks, so they managed. Mickey's mother, Sherry Grimsley, helped too. Just a few days before, she had bought him a complete set of school clothes and had given him some spending money. Mickey had learned not to count on much help from his father. When Larry Gene wasn't in jail, he had his second family, a wife and two small children to worry about. As a youngster, Mickey had grown up attending a branch of a fundamentalist church, the Assemblies of God, where he had been taught to respect God and fear the Devil. He loved music. He liked Steve Perry, but was a fervid Ozzy Ozbourne fan. In his pocket that day was a $11.50 general admission ticket for a Wednesday night Ozzy

Ozbourne concert. There were also concert tickets for Ratt, a rock group, at the municipal auditorium in Nashville, and a KDF Radio Station club membership card.

Then Larry Gene's truck came up the street. It was a four wheel drive, yellow vehicle with oversize tires. "There they are now," Granny said. "Looks like your cousin Kenny is with your daddy."

The truck passed the house and stopped a short distance down the road. Mickey jumped down from the front porch and trotted down to his father's truck. His grandmother saw them talking for a few minutes, then Mickey got in the truck with his father and cousin.

Kenny Summers was the son of Larry Gene's sister, Pauline, and her husband, Carl Douglas Summers, who was known to his family and friends as Billy Summers. Kenny had five brothers and one sister. Like his first cousin Mickey, Kenny was a few months into his seventeenth year. Mickey had turned seventeen in May. Kenny's birthday was in June. Unlike Mickey, Kenny was no longer in school. He had quit high school after a disagreement with the principal. But Kenny had ambitions. He had decided to get his high school diploma by taking a GED exam, and then, when he was eighteen, he had big plans to go to vocational school and become an electrician. He had told his grandmother, "Nanny, I am gonna go over there and learn to be an electrician and when I do that, you won't have a thing in the world to worry about. I will make you a living."

His mother had remarked, "That is something Kenny and Larry Gene had in common. They would give anybody the last thing they had."

Since quitting high school, Kenny earned money mowing yards. He had a regular list of customers. In the garage were several old lawn mowers. Kenny had a mechanical ability to swap parts and make repairs so he could keep his favorite mower purring along in top condition.

That day, September 3, in spite of a sore knee, Kenny had been busy with his yard-mowing jobs. He was back home early in the afternoon and took a shower. Kenny kept himself scrupulously clean.

After his shower, Kenny put on white Fruit of the Loom underwear, then stepped into a pair of new Levi blue jeans. They had a tear in one knee that his mother had darned. The shirt he chose was pale blue with red and white stripes. Finally, he put on a pair of brown leather loafers and reached for his red cap. In his pocket was a pocket knife, his most prized possession, given to him by his father. The two things most important to Kenny were his cap and his knife. He liked to wear his cap at a jaunty angle, tilted to one side. When he stepped outside, he was about a mile and a half from his grandmother Thaxton's house where his cousin Mickey lived.

It was shortly after three O'clock that afternoon of September 3, when his uncle Larry Gene pulled up in his four-wheel drive truck. He leaned out of the window.

"Hi, Kenny. C'mon over here."

"Hi, Uncle Larry." Kenny had loved his uncle ever since he was a youngster and Uncle Larry stuffed his pockets with candy. He thought Larry Gene was a neat guy, always fun to be around, always cooking up some crazy scheme. The fact that some of those schemes had landed Larry in jail didn't bother Kenny too much. He just thought Larry Gene Jones was a man who was brave enough to live life on his own terms. Besides, Larry Gene's relatives were a tight-knit clan. If one of them got in trouble, they stuck together.

"C'mon, get in the truck," Larry Gene said with one of his

reckless grins. "I'm settin' here waiting for Mickey. You seen him today?"

"No, I ain' t seen him."

"Well, his granny said he'd be along soon, so I reckon he'll show up any time now."

Kenny went around and got into the truck from the other side. As soon as he got in the truck, he smelled liquor. A half empty bottle was on the seat beside Larry Gene. He could tell that Larry Gene had been drinking heavily. He also sensed a feeling of tension and excitement in the air. His uncle was tapping his fingers nervously on the steering wheel to the rhythm of a loud country western tune on the radio."I wish that boy would hurry up and git home," Larry Gene said impatiently.

"Oh, there he is now!" He saw Mickey talking to Inez on the front porch. The old woman pointed toward the truck.

Larry Gene honked the horn and started the engine. He drove a little distance past the house and stopped again.

"I want to talk to Mickey alone without his granny hearing us," he explained.

Curiosity was making Kenny excited. Something important was up. He felt adventure in the air. Mickey trotted over to the truck. His insides lit up like a light bulb being switched on when he saw his dad. He idolized his Larry Gene. He wanted to be like him. He was, like his cousin Kenny, blinded to his father's shortcomings by the spell of the Larry Gene Jones charm.

"Get in here, son. I want you to help me with something."
"Sure, Dad." Mickey went around and joined his cousin in the truck cab. "We goin' some place?" Larry Gene chuckled. "Tell you in a minute." He turned the truck around, paused to say something to Mickey's grandmother who was on the front

porch watching them, then gunned the truck and pulled away in a cloud of dust. Mickey took out his pack of cigarettes, offered one to his cousin, then shook out one for himself. Both boys, regular smokers, lit up. Mickey drew in a lungful of smoke. "You boys want a snort?" Larry Gene invited, gesturing to the bottle on the seat beside him. "Help yourselves." Mickey laughed with the exuberance of a teenager throwing off the confines of boring school routine. This was what he loved about his renegade father. Larry Gene Jones was a modern outlaw, always out to have a good time and thumb his nose at authority figures. Kenny felt the same way. He'd had his own run-in with stuffy school rules and regulations. To hell with them all.

Kenny had a pull at the bottle, blinked, managed not to have a choking spell, wiped the neck with his sleeve and handed it to Mickey who also swallowed some of the fiery liquid.

It was an afternoon of teenage rebellion and Larry Gene Jones was a pied piper leading the way.

"Where we goin', Dad?" Mickey asked as he saw they were driving out of town.

"We're goin' down to Trousdale County and steal us a truckload of marijuana. Top-grade stuff. Sinsemilla."

Mickey felt a clutch of fear and excitement in his stomach. "Where in Trousdale County?"

"Jerry Ward's place. Boys, he's got himself a crop of the best grass I've seen in a long time. And I seen it myself. I was almost close enough last week to get my hands on it. Me and Curt Fishburn snuck over onto the Ward place last week. Jerry Ward's growing it behind a big fence alongside the barn. I was gonna get me a sample, till that wife of hissen, Melinda, run us off with a shotgun. Anyway, I figure by now they've cut some of the stuff and got it stashed in the barn.':

Mickey had a prickly sensation all over. "How're we gonna get it out of their barn?"

"We'll just go help ourselves, that's how. You know what a truckload of that top-grade maryjane is worth? A bunch. Maybe like ten thousand dollars. And the Wards sure as hell cain't go to the law, complainin' that we took their marijuana, now can they?"

That much money dazzled Mickey's imagination. He could see himself driving to school in a bright red sports car, bought with his share of the money. It made sense that once they got away with the truckload of marijuana, the Wards couldn't do a blessed thing about it, since they were breaking the law in the first place by raising the stuff. It wasn't like holding up a bank where you'd have the law down on your neck afterwards. Still, his father's plan had something of a dream-like quality. Mickey asked the practical question.

"What are we goin' to do about the Wards? Jerry Ward ain't goin' to just stand around and let us back up to his barn and help ourselves."

"You leave that up to me," Larry Gene grinned. "Look back there."

The boys twisted around. Behind the seat, they saw an old shotgun and a pistol. A chilly sensation made their hearts pound. "You figure on shootin' Jerry Ward?" Mickey asked.

Larry Gene laughed. "Nothin' like that. I'll do what Melinda did last week when she run us off the place. I'll shoot up in the air a couple of times, stick the gun in Jerry Ward's face, and scare the hell out of him. You let me take care of the Wards. What I need you boys for is to help me load that marijuana in the truck, once't I run Jerry and Melinda off. I can't load all that stuff by myself. Won't be nothin' for two husky youngsters like you. We can shoo off Jerry and Melinda, load up the truck, and be off that place in fifteen minutes. I got it all figured out."

The plan seemed to make a whole lot better sense to Mickey now. Larry Gene took another swig from the bottle, turned up the radio volume, and the three of them started singing loudly along with Roy Clark. They were off on what promised to be a great adventure.

Chapter 2

Earlier that morning, a major player was being propelled into the day's developing horror. At 7:30a.m., forty-two year old Howard Collins started the engine of a flatbed truck and drove out of Centerville, Tennessee. His destination was a metal storage building on the Ward property south of Hartsville. On the side of the cab of the flatbed truck was the lettering, "Ward Construction Company." Being pulled by the truck was a utility trailer for hauling heavy equipment. It was destined to play a part in the bloody events later that day. Riding beside Howard Collins in the cab of the truck was Hubert Ward Jr., father of Jerry Lawrence Ward.

Some individuals seize life and by sheer willpower ,cleverness, or determination manage to shape events somewhat to their desire. Others are overwhelmed by life, shoved here and there, struggling to keep their heads above water with little or no say in their destiny. Howard Collins was such a person. If he had known what lay in store for him that day, he might have bolted from the truck and not stopped running for a week. But this was another current that was sucking his life into an unwanted vortex, and in keeping with the pattern of his life, he seemed to have little control of his fate.

Collins was born in Pensacola, Florida. He was at cross purposes with life from the beginning. He never knew his real father. He knew his mother but did not live with her. He was raised by stepparents. He did not get along well with his stepfather. His high school career came to an abrupt end in the eleventh grade when he had a disagreement with his teacher and principal. He walked out of the school never to return, although he did later get a GED equivalent high school diploma.

Life did not hold many successes for Howard Collins. After leaving high school, he worked for a while in a filling station, then for a year in his stepfather's clock business. A brief stint in the armed forces gave him a break in a drab existence. He was stationed in Germany on the East German and Czech border. Back in Alabama after being honorably discharged from the army, Collins drifted into construction work as a laborer and continued from then on to earn his living at that trade. He married and had two sons. The marriage ended in divorce.

The dark fate that was to involve Howard Collins in the day's events began several months earlier with his getting a job in Pensacola, Florida, at a construction site at a railroad yard.

His girlfriend's mother worked at the county health center in Pensacola. She knew Howard was looking for a job. Through a friend she had heard about the construction site at the railroad yard. She told Howard about it, and he applied for a job. The second morning that he showed up there, he was put to work.

The construction company he went to work for was Reinhart and Ward. The person in charge of the Reinhart and Ward job in Pensacola was Hubert Ward Jr. Like a piece on a chessboard, Collins was moved by fate into the square occupied by Hubert Ward Jr., and from then on, his life was intertwined with that of the senior Ward. They worked together on construction sites, and on September 3, 1985, they drove in the truck together to the farm where Jerry Ward lived.

They had been working on a construction job in Centerville, Tennessee for a week. They were taking the truck and utility trailer to the storage shed on the Ward farm to pick up pipe fitting supplies and forms. Collins and the senior Ward drove through Hartsville, taking highway 141 south, and arrived at the Ward farm early in the afternoon. Collins backed the truck around and pulled to the side of the storage shed. At that point they were across the road from Grace Ward's house.

Collins and Jerry Ward's father consulted a three-page list of supplies that were needed and began sorting through forms and pipe fittings stacked beside the fence.

It was a hot, quiet late summer afternoon. No breeze stirred. The corn stalks and high weeds on the Ward farm were as still as shapes on a painted canvas. Above them, the sun was bright in a cloudless sky. Howard Collins was sweating as he shoved the heavy forms around. He didn't mind. His muscles were conditioned to hard work.

They had been working for about an hour when Howard suddenly heard a truck engine being loudly revved up. He stopped what he was doing and looked around. He glanced at Hubert Jr., who also had stopped to listen.

"What the heck is that?" Howard asked.

"Beats me."

"Sounds like there's a truck over there on Jerry's place."

"I don't know what Jerry'd be doing with a truck making that kind of racket."

The tall weeds across the road hid from sight whatever was going on.

The senior Hubert shrugged and went back to work. They were interrupted again, this time by loud shouting coming from some distance down the road. Howard jumped down from the truck. Hubert Jr. dropped a pipe fitting. They both hurried out to the road.

A startling sight met their eyes. Jerry Ward and his wife Melinda were standing in the road, hollering loudly. Howard couldn't make out what they were saying.

"Something's wrong," Hubert Jr. exclaimed. "C'mon." The

two men ran to where Jerry and Melinda were standing. As they got closer, Howard saw that Jerry Ward was covered with blood. All he was wearing was a pair of shorts. His legs were bloody. He turned and pointed to his back, which was streaked with blood. Melinda was sobbing hysterically.

"What's happened, son?" the senior Ward demanded. Jerry was so agitated he could hardly speak. His words came out in an almost incoherent rush. ''1 was up at Mother's house. Three men came up to the house. They threatened to kill me and Mother. They shot me. I knocked the biggest man down and grabbed his gun. I ran across the field between the house and the trailer and got Melinda."

"How'd you get all bloody like that?"

"I told you, I've been shot."

"Who were the men? Do you know them? Do you know what they want?"

"No."

Hubert Jr. looked upset and angry. "Howard, you go unhook the trailer from the truck."

Collins ran back up the hill and struggled with the trailer hitch. By the time he got it unhooked, Jerry and Hubert had gotten there.

"Get in the truck," Hubert ordered. "We're going to drive down to the house and find out what the hell is going on down there."

Howard was a man used to taking orders. Without questioning Hubert's command or thinking about what he might be getting himself into, he obediently started the truck. Looking back to the horrible events of that afternoon, Howard Collins was to say later, "If I knew then what I know now, I would have jumped in that truck fast and drove right on off down that road before any guns had been brought out. At that point, though, I thought what I was doing was helping my boss and his family protect their home against three intruders I'd never seen. According to what Jerry said, it was three men who had come up and tried to force their way into the house. Later, I found out it was really a man and two teenage boys.

"One thing that struck me as kind of strange, although I didn't give it much thought at the time, was Jerry saying that these people had shot at him, and that he'd been shot. When Hubert and I were on the hill at the storage shed, we should have been able to hear if any shots had been fired. Sounds out in the country that way travel a long distance. We never heard any shots, only the sound of the truck engine revving up two or three times. As for Jerry saying he'd been shot, I didn't see anything that looked like a bullet wound on him, and he didn't ask to be taken to a doctor. He later told Thomas East that he'd cut himself running through the weeds and briars. That's where all that blood on him came from."

Jerry and Hubert got in the cab beside Collins. Howard backed and turned the truck. At that point he noticed that Jerry was holding a small, black pistol, a revolver with a white handle. Jerry said, "This is the gun I took away from the guy who came up on Mother's porch."

Howard drove to within thirty feet of the house and parked in the drive. As they got out of the truck, Jerry handed Howard a different pistol. This one was chromeplated with a black handle, a .32 caliber.

Hubert said, "Y'all wait here. I'm going to get some more guns."

Hubert got behind the wheel of the truck and pulled out of the yard. Jerry said, "Howard, you go around and watch the back of the house and I'll stay here and watch the front."

Howard felt an edge of fear. The perspiration on his forehead was not entirely from the heat. At the same time, he was keyed up and excited. He didn't know what was going on, but he did not question the increasing role he was playing in this drama. He was blindly loyal to the Wards. He had a world of respect for his boss, Hubert Ward Jr. He said Hubert had taught him more about operating heavy equipment and reading blueprints than any schooling he'd gotten on previous jobs.

Whatever was going on, at that point, he took their side and did what he was told to do. He thought he was doing the right thing, helping protect law-abiding people from dangerous criminals who had invaded their property.

Howard stood back of the house for a while. Then he heard voices around front He moved to the corner of the house and saw Jerry talking to another man. At the time, Howard did not know the man. Later, he found out the man was Kenneth Scruggs, a friend of the Wards. Jerry had seen him driving by and had flagged him down, asking for his help. Scruggs was holding a shotgun. Collins joined the two men. Ward and Scruggs decided to go into the house to see if the intruders were in there.

Jerry said, "I've got a machine gun in the house. I have to get it."

They told, Collins to wait outside. He stayed to the left of the front porch. After a few minutes, Scruggs and Ward came back out.

"Nobody's in there," Jerry said. Howard saw that Jerry was now carrying an automatic weapon that looked like some kind of machine gun. It was a rapid fire .45 caliber rifle called a "spitfire."

At that point, Hubert Ward Jr. returned, driving the flatbed truck into the yard. He got out of the cab and brought out three shotguns, handing one to Collins. Howard stuck the pistol

Jerry had given into a back pocket. Suddenly, a truck engine started up. It sounded as if it were in the area of the chicken yard back near the barn.

"They're stealing my game roosters!" Jerry exclaimed. Howard and the other three men, all now armed, ran back to the chicken yard. They saw that a gate had been knocked down as if it had been rammed. The truck engine roared again. Now they realized that the truck was not in the chicken yard. The racket was coming from behind a high wall near the large tobacco barn that was some distance behind the farmhouse. Howard saw the tracks the truck had made through the tall weeds from the smashed gate to the walled area beside the barn.

Jerry Ward, Kenneth Scruggs, Hubert Ward Jr., and Howard Collins were scattered out in the field a number of yards apart. Some distance behind them was Jerry's wife, Melinda. She, too, was holding a gun.

When Larry Gene Jones had pulled into the Ward driveway earlier that hot afternoon, Mickey was sitting on the edge of the truck seat, his body tense. His fists were clenched and he felt his heart racing with excitement.

At first everything had gone according to Larry Gene's reckless plan. They had thrown a scare into Jerry Ward and his wife and chased them off the property. Then Larry Gene had driven around the house, across the yard, past the long row of gamecock cages.

There, they were confronted with a fence made of posts And wire. Larry Gene stopped the truck and took a long pull at his bottle of liquor. He wiped the back of his hand across his mouth, raked the four-wheel drive vehicle into low gear, let out a loud "Whoop!" and plunged right into the fence, knocking down a gate. Mickey and Kenneth were both laughing and yelling with excitement. The truck plowed a swath through a field of six-foot high corn stalks and weeds on the way to the barn.

Mickey saw the high wooden wall his father had described. It surrounded an area on the side of the barn. This was where the marijuana was grown. Without hesitating, Larry Gene drove into the wall, smashing his way through to the barn. The air was filled with the sound of roaring truck engine, whining gears, and splintering lumber.

Then Larry Gene pulled up to the barn. As he'd suspected, part of the marijuana crop had been harvested and stacked in the barn.

"All right," Jones yelled to the boys. "Get it loaded into the truck!"

A high level of adrenalin was coursing through Mickey's blood stream. He felt extra strong. He worked fast beside Kenny, heaving marijuana into the truck bed. The dusty air burned Mickey's nostrils and made him cough.

Larry Gene drained the rest of the liquor. By then he was staggering. "That's enough," he told the boys. "Now let's get outa here!"

He stumbled into the truck, started up the engine, and backed out into the field. Over the noise the truck was making, Mickey heard two shots. He felt a sudden stab of apprehension. He twisted around in the seat, trying to see where the shots had come from.

Larry Gene kept backing wildly; the truck bounced over rows in the corn field and crashed through a low fence. When the shots rang out, Howard Collins later said, he thought it sounded like a rifle and a shotgun. He didn't know who fired the shots. When he heard the gunfire, Howard hit the ground. From his position on the ground, Collins raised his head. A startling sight met his eyes. A yellow pickup truck was backing out over a section of flattened wall-like fence near the barn. Evidently, the driver had knocked down the wall to get - into the area near the barn and was now backing out.

As the truck came bouncing and surging backward over the rough ground toward the fence, a fusillade of shots rang out. The truck backed some thirty feet from the barn. Lead sang through the hot summer afternoon as guns blazed away. Howard, up on his feet now, fired his shotgun once in the direction of the truck.

The truck kept backing up, crashing through the corn and weeds. Then there was a clashing, raking sound of gears being meshed as the driver attempted to change direction and go forward. Something had gone wrong. The truck engine roared at high speed, but the truck would not move. The clatter of gunfire mingled with the tortured whine of the stalled truck. The air was filled with the smell of burned gunpowder.

In the truck, Larry Gene Jones was cursing as he struggled with the jammed gears. Kenny and Mickey had both turned pale. Mickey felt his stomach twist into a cold, tight knot. All of a sudden, this was no longer a fun adventure. Something had gone terribly wrong. He saw several men in the Ward farmyard with guns, shooting at them. Bullets were hitting the truck, some making a whining sound as they ricocheted off the metal.

Larry Gene struck the steering wheel of the stalled truck with frustration.

Swearing, he reached behind the seat and grabbed his old shotgun. There was a pause in the shooting. Larry Gene Jones opened his door and stepped to the ground. He leveled the shotgun through the open window of the truck. Howard Collins had fired his shotgun again. There were no more shots left in his gun. He saw the driver of the truck point a shotgun through an open window of the truck. There was a puff of smoke and a loud "bang!" Hot pain stung Howard's right arm. The shock knocked Collins to the ground. He was aware of several more shots and then the shooting stopped. Someone yelled to the occupants of the truck to get out and walk to the fence.

Instead, the driver got back into the truck and again tried to get the gears to mesh, but the truck would not move. There were more shouted orders for the truck occupants to leave the truck and walk to the fence with their hands up. Clutching his right arm that had been struck by a shotgun pellet, Howard got to his feet and joined in the yelling.

In the truck, Mickey wanted to beg his father to get them out of there, but panic had frozen his vocal cords. Larry Gene struggled a bit more with the truck, then gave up. "Ain't no use, boys. I cain't get this damn thing to move. We'd best do as they say and get out and walk over to the fence." Mickey exchanged frightened looks with his cousin. Their big adventure wasn't supposed to turn out this way. The afternoon had turned deadly serious.

"What do you reckon they'll do to us?" Kenny asked in an unsteady voice.

"Aw, hell, they won't do nothin'," Larry Gene blustered. "They're in trouble with the law already, growin' a crop of marijuana like this. I'll talk to them."

Jones got out of the truck and started toward the fence with his hands up. The situation had done little to sober him up.

He weaved and stumbled as he walked. He was grinning in a disarming manner .

Mickey felt numb all over as he followed his father to the waist-high wire fence that separated them from the grim faced men pointing guns at them. There was a cold feeling in the pit of his stomach. He wondered where all the men and guns had come from. There had only been Jerry Ward and his wife on the farm when the Jones' truck got there ˝less than an hour ago. Now Mickey saw three or four men beside Jerry's wife. They were all heavily armed.

Howard Collins saw that the driver of the truck who had shot at him was a tall man. He was surprised to see that the other two were just teenage boys.

The boys came across the fence when they were told to do so. The man, however, said he couldn't get over the fence. Hubert fired a shot in the air. The man awkwardly scrambled over the fence, losing a shoe in the process. He made an attempt to retrieve the shoe, but was ordered to leave it where it had fallen.

At the time, Howard Collins did not know who the man and the two boys were. Later, he was to learn their identities. It looked to Howard as if the man, Larry Gene, was spaced-out or intoxicated. He didn't appear to be frightened by the situation. He just grinned in a disarming way.

Afterwards, Howard remembered how Larry Gene tried to talk his way out of the situation.

Jones had said, "Look here, fellers, why don't we just forget this whole thing? All we done was to come here to get some of your marijuana. Shucks, you got plenty. The little bit we took won't hurt you none. Tell you what, let's forget all about this and I'll help repair that barn wall we knocked down and I'll fix the gate and fence we damaged. Why don't we just unload this marijuana and forget about what happened and let us go on our way and just be happy."

Marijuana.

The word sent a cold shiver down Howard Collins' spine.

Suddenly this situation was taking on an entirely new and sinister meaning. Up to now, Collins thought he was helping his employer and family protect their home against people who had come to rob or harm them. Instead, he now found he had innocently gotten himself embroiled in a deadly battle over illegal marijuana. He was filled with a new kind of apprehension that would grow with each passing minute.

Hubert was yelling at the intruders in a loud, angry voice. "What the hell do you mean coming onto my property, Threatening to kill my son and threatening to kill my ex-wife?"

Larry Gene Jones said, "I just done that to throw a scare into Jerry there so's he'd leave and we could get the marijuana, that's all."

During this time, the boys had been silent. They looked pale and frightened. Mickey cleared his throat. "My...my dad picked us up after school and wanted us to come along."

The confrontation was taking place in the chicken coop area, some fifteen feet from the fence that Larry Gene and the two boys had crossed. Howard glanced around. Jerry Ward was standing to his right. Hubert was positioned near the end of the fence. For the first time Howard became aware that Melinda Ward was also present. She was standing some distance behind Jerry and Collins. She was holding a shotgun.

At this point, Kenneth Scruggs spoke up. "Jerry, don't you reckon we should call the police?" Jerry scowled at him. "We can't call the police. There's marijuana out here."

There was a strained silence. For a moment Scruggs didn't say anything. He looked around at the two frightened boys, at the men and the woman holding the guns. Then he said,

"Well, then I'm leaving."

He walked away, leaving Howard and the Wards guarding

Larry Gene Jones and the two boys. By then it was about five 0'clock in the afternoon.

Howard's arm was throbbing, but the wound did not appear to be serious. He wiped the blood from his arm on his trousers. He was too frightened to worry much about the flesh wound from the shotgun pellet. He told Jerry that he was out of ammunition.

"Go get some more," Jerry ordered. "There's some in the shed in front of the barn. Look on the shelf just inside the door."

Howard went to the shed and got five shells. He put three in his shotgun and gave Hubert the other two. Then he walked back to where he had been standing. The tension he felt was becoming unbearable.

Jerry came over, took Howard's shotgun, and gave him the automatic rifle.

The boys were standing still, their hands clasped on their heads.

Larry Gene Jones lowered his hands. Hubert yelled, "You get them hands up, and you keep them up. Don't you drop them again!"

Jones let his hands drop. Instantly, Hubert fired. Larry Gene fell to the ground, clutching his right arm below the wrist. He cried out in pain.

"Get up!" Hubert ordered, menacing the fallen man with his rifle.

"I cain't get up," Jones moaned. Mickey was filled with horror. With tearful, stricken eyes, he looked at his fallen father. He lowered his hands and tried to reach down to help his father.

Hubert swung his rifle toward Mickey. "You get them hands back up, boy! You keep them on top of your head where I can see them!"

Mickey obeyed. Howard Collins felt a wave of pity for the boy who wanted so desperately to help his wounded father. After some ten minutes, Larry Gene was able to get back on his feet. It appear to Howard that he had only been shot in the hand. The wound did not appear serious.

Larry Gene was clutching his hand, looking around at his captors. It looked to Howard as if Jones was trying to make a decision. He shot a glance toward the fence and the barn area. He moistened his lips. Suddenly, he turned and began running toward the barn. Hubert raised the barrel of his gun in one quick motion and, without taking aim, fired.

Larry Gene fell near the fence, screaming in pain. He rolled around, soaking the ground with blood. "Oh, God, I'm shot. I'm shot real bad!" he sobbed. "Mickey, please come help me, son! Get a doctor!"

With a cry of anguish, Mickey started toward his wounded father.

There was a shouted order from Hubert for him to freeze. "You stop right there, boy, or you'll get the same dose of lead I gave your old man." He pointed his gun at Mickey. Until now, Mickey had tried to keep up a brave and manly front in spite of how frightened he was. But the sight of his wounded father on the ground, pleading for help, was too much. He couldn't hold back his tears. "Please, mister," he begged. "Let me help him."

"You do what I tell you. You stand right there and keep your hands on your head."

"But he's hurt real bad. Please get a doctor." Mickey's pleas fell on deaf ears. He was forced to stand helplessly by while his father moaned in pain and pleaded for Mickey to come help him. Grief and anger raged through Mickey as he saw that his father's shirt was soaked with blood. Memories of all the good times they'd had together tore at his heart. Mickey didn't care what people said about Larry Gene Jones, about him being irresponsible and always getting in trouble. He'd been a wonderful dad with his laughing, generous ways. Mickey couldn't even blame him for the trouble they were in now. They hadn't done anything all that terrible. Hadn't his dad offered to repair the damage they'd done to the fence and barn? There wasn't any reason to shoot him down in cold blood and leave him lying there like he was nothing but a dog.

"Please let me help my dad," Mickey begged again. Hubert said, "Jerry, go get some rope and tie them bastards up."

Jerry went to the barn. He brought a roll of rope. Hubert grasped a section of the rope and tested it with a hard jerk. The rope snapped in two. "This stuff's rotten," Hubert said disgustedly, throwing the pieces away. "Get something stronger."

Jerry went back to the shed and returned with a roll of electric fence wire and a pair of wire pliers. He took the automatic weapon from Howard and ordered him to tie up the boys.

By now Collins had lost the stomach for this situation. He was sorry he'd gotten involved. He wished fervently that he could somehow get away from there. But after the violence he had just witnessed, he was in the clutches of a growing fear for his own life. The casual way Hubert had shot the Jones man showed Collins that he was surrounded by dangerous and violent people. If he wanted to stay alive, he knew he had no choice; he had to cooperate with the Ward family.

Reluctantly, Howard obeyed Jerry's order. Using the wire and pliers, he tied the hands of the boys behind them, spaced about seven or eight inches apart, and he tied their feet together, As Collins was tying them, Mickey, making a valiant effort not to break down, asked Howard in a trembling voice,

"What are they going to do to us?"

Collins replied in a low voice, "Young man, I work for this man in construction. I had no idea that any of this was going to happen. I have no idea what they're going to do to you. If you know how to pray, that's what I would do if I were you. That's all I can tell you, son."

Howard Collins was a God-fearing man. He had been raised in the Baptist faith. He considered himself a law abiding man and a Christian. Later, he was to remark bitterly,

"I can't understand why God allowed me to get involved in something this terrible. I've only been in trouble once before in my life, after my divorce when I took my two little boys against court orders out of what I thought was a bad family situation."

After being tied, the two boys were ordered to get down on their knees. Putting his weight on his injured knee caused Kenny a great deal of pain. "I got a hurt knee," he said. "Can I stand up?"

"You stay right there, you son of a bitch." They remained kneeling for the rest of the afternoon. Mickey's father, gasping with pain, made several attempts to get up, but Hubert hollered in a loud voice for him to stay down.

Hubert Ward then ordered Howard to tie up Larry Gene the same as he had tied the boys. Howard did as he was told, tying Jones' hands behind his back and his feet together.

"It was very regrettable that I had to tie up those boys and his father that way, but at that point I was trying to stay alive myself," Collins later said.

Howard stood up and started to walk away, but Hubert yelled, "Tie him several times."

Howard walked back and put more wire around the fallen man's hands and feet.

Then Howard started to walk back to where he had originally been standing, but Hubert hollered at him to stay where he was, near the captives.

The wounded man was making a lot of racket, crying out in pain, begging for help, trying to talk. "Oh, Lord God," he sobbed. "Oh, sweet Jesus, please help me. I'm hurt bad. I'm hurt so bad inside somewhere. Please, please in God's name, somebody help me. Get me to a doctor....'!

"Dammit to hell, I can't stand no more of your bellyaching!" Jerry Ward swore. He came over, grasped a fistful of Larry Gene Jones' hair, jerked his head back, and crammed a bandana in his mouth, gagging him. Then he stood up and kicked the fallen man very hard in the left shoulder.

After that, the only sound from Larry Gene were muffled sobs and groans. Mickey didn't know how it was possible to feel so much fear and grief and hate all at once. He couldn't bear to look at his bound and gagged father writhing on the ground in agony. He was consumed by hatred for these men who were treating his father like an animal. At the same time, fear for his own life was making him numb. When he looked at his cousin Kenny's pale face, he saw the same deathly fear, although Kenny kept stoically silent.

Shadows from the barn and chicken coops were beginning to lengthen as twilight approached.

Howard saw the Wards, Hubert, Jerry, and Melinda, off at a distance, conferring among themselves. Hubert would disappear a while, and be gone a fairly good time, and then he would show back up and they'd talk a little more and he'd disappear again.

Collins didn't know what was going on. He was in a cold sweat, wondering if he was going to come out of this alive. He felt sure they must be talking about him too, wondering what to do about him. Now he knew about the marijuana, about the shooting. He could be a dangerous witness. He had never before in his life been so scared.

He was too frightened to make any kind of a move other than to just go along and hope to God they didn't turn on him. At one point he was sure they were discussing him because they would go up on the hill a distance away from him to talk and they'd look over at him and go back to talking again. They did that two or three times. Collins wondered if they were deciding if they'd better do away with him so there wouldn't be any witnesses.

By then it had grown dark. Howard walked up the hill to the house. He saw that the company truck had been moved since they drove it into the yard earlier that afternoon.

As Howard was waiting at the company truck, a man walked toward him, coming from the direction of the house. The man was carrying a bottle of beer. "I am drunk," he said. "They call me 'Little Hubert The Third,' and I'm drunk."

Collins later said, "The name 'Little Hubert' sure didn't describe him. He looked like a big, hairy bear. He had a flashlight under his chin, shining up on his face. He scared the hell out of me because he was so big and rough." Hubert stuck his huge hand out and said, "Daddy told me what all you've done for us. I want to thank you, and I'll take care of you." His father, the older Hubert, walked up. "Get the hell out of the way," he told his son. "We've got work to do." It was obvious to Howard that there was no question about what Little Hubert said regarding the state of his intoxication. He was, as the saying goes, "drunk as a skunk."

Howard later learned that Hubert the Third was Jerry's brother. There were three Ward sons: Jerry Lawrence, Hubert III and Bobby. They had one sister, Byrdie. For reasons known only to the family, the father, Hubert Jr. was called "Big Hubert" and Hubert III was called "Little Hubert," despite the fact that "Little Hubert" was a much larger man than "Big Hubert."

Big Hubert, the father, and Little Hubert had a brief conversation and Little Hubert headed back toward the house, walking unsteadily.

Collins walked back to where the two boys were still kneeling in the dirt. He heard Mickey ask, "What are you all going to do to us?"

Big Hubert, the father, said, "We got to wait for the big man to show up. He'll decide what to do."

Chapter 3

September 4, 1985

At a cafe across the street from a newspaper office in Macon County, Jake Nixon was sitting on a counter stool, having apple pie a la mode with a double dip of ice cream to top off a meal of juicy sirloin steak. He finished dessert with his fifth cup of coffee and fifteenth cigarette for the day. Jake was not one to waste time worrying about cholesterol and blood pressure.

At forty years of age, Jake Nixon was divorced; he had suffered the tragic loss of a son killed by a drunk driver; his only other child, a daughter, had grown up to become a stranger. Jake was sufficiently disillusioned with life not to want to take heroic measures to extend it beyond a reasonable boundary.

Jake described himself as a cheerful cynic. He did not consider himself soured on life, merely bitterly amused by it. People liked him, probably because he took a keen interest in what they had to say. But more than that, running contrary to the somewhat hard-boiled cynical streak because of the blows life had dealt in his own life, there was in Jake Nixon a genuine compassion and sympathy for the people he wrote about.

Somewhere he had read, "Be kind, for everyone you meet is fighting a hard battle." Jake believed that. He'd seen enough of life to know that everyone he saw was carrying some kind of private cross or silent grief. As for himself, he had never gotten over the loss of his son. That compassion for the people he wrote about was what made him a good human interest reporter.

"Hi, Jake."

He looked up as a fellow reporter slid onto the stool next to him. This cafe was a favorite hangout for newspaper people. Most of them spent their lunch and coffee breaks here. "City editor wants to see you when you get back to the newsroom," the reporter said.

"Okay," Jake replied, arising from the stool.

"How's the meat loaf today?" "It's edible." Jake dropped a dollar bill beside his empty plate, stopped at the register to pay his bill, then crossed the busy street to the newspaper building.

He had never entirely adjusted to the atmosphere of a modern newsroom. When he'd started his newspaper career, the newsroom was filled with the clatter of typewriters. These days, reporters and copy writers worked at silent computer terminals. The silence was deafening.

Jake tapped at the glass door of the city editor's office, opened it and looked in. "Bill Jenkins said you wanted to see me?"

"Yeah, Jake," Hal Bevans said. "C'mon, in." Jake entered the office, took a seat near the desk, and shook a fresh cigarette out of a crumpled pack.

"Jake, what the hell are you doing? You know the no smoking rules in here."

"Oh, yeah. I keep forgetting. Okay if I just suck on it without lighting it?"

Hal laughed. "I don't think they've got any rules about that. Anyway, this is why I called you in. We got a tip from someone in the sheriff's department that three fellows who live in Lafayette are missing. Actually, I think it's a man and two teenage boys. I don't think it's officially a missing person case yet. I don't know if there's a story in it or not. Might be a wild goose chase, but I thought you'd better check into it."

"Okay. Who are these people?"

Bevans handed him a slip of paper. "This is the name and address of the grandmother of the boys. You could start there."

Jake left the office. Outside, in the parking lot, he slid behind the wheel of his eight-year old Ford, careful not to touch metal heated by the blazing afternoon sun. The dents, rust spots, and worn upholstery made the car look all of its eight years. So did the speedometer, which had passed the 100,000 mile mark 10,000miles ago. Jake was perspiring before he got his key in the ignition lock. He wished the air conditioner worked.

He drove to a modest frame house on a quiet street, the address given to him by his editor.

Inez Thaxton lived on Oak Street about 200 feet from the main road running through Lafayette. The house was probably built in the '40s or '50s. It was a plain, two story, weatherboard house, painted yellow, with a small yard. It was situated across the street from a government housing project. Many of the people who lived in the housing project came from substandard houses that at one time lined Oak Street. Those houses were gone now and empty lots stood as a reminder of the past. The Thaxton house had the kitchen and living quarters on the ground floor. The bedrooms were on the second floor.

The house was modestly furnished with older furniture, but kept in neat order. The kitchen was kept spotlessly clean. The only thing that annoyed Inez Thaxton about the house were the mice. She claimed her mice jumped around like miniature kangaroos . Jake parked in front of the house, walked up to the porch, and knocked at the front door.

A woman appeared behind the screen door. She was short, a bit over five feet, but weighed all of two hundred pounds. Her hair was dark brown, her eyes green. She was in her mid-60s. She peered at Jake through her bifocals. "Yes?"

"Are you Mrs. Inez Thaxton?"

"Yes. Who are you?"

"I'm Jake Nixon, Ma'am. I'm from the newspaper. We heard your grandsons are missing. I wonder if I could talk to you for a few minutes."

Well, sure you can. Come on in." She opened the screen door.

Jake entered the living room area. His reporter's training for details took in at a glance the worn, inexpensive furnishings. He judged that Inez Thaxton was a woman living on an extremely restricted budget.

Now that Jake was in the room and had a better look at her, it was obvious that she was extremely agitated and worried. Her hands were nervous and restless. She appeared to be on the verge of tears.

"Please have a seat, Mr. Nixon." Jake settled into an old easy chair with frayed arms and sagging springs.

Inez Thaxton sat on a worn couch that looked like a Goodwill markdown. Jake said, "I understand that the missing boys are your grandsons."

"Yes ,Kenny and Mickey. His father is my son, Larry Gene Jones. He's missing too. Kenny is Mickey's cousin, Kenneth Summers. The three of them drove off yesterday after Mickey got home from school. Mickey promised he wouldn't be gone long. But they didn't come home last night and they still haven't come home. We're just all worried sick."

"Do you have any idea where they might have gone?" She shook her head. "No, I don't. I'll tell you the truth, Mr. Nixon, my boy, Larry Gene, has gotten into scrapes most of his life. I done my best to raise him right, but he just can't seem to stay out of trouble. In spite of that, Larry Gene has a real sweet, generous side to his nature. Everybody in the family loves

him, and his boy Mickey just worships him. Still, I just don't
know what Larry Gene might have gotten those boys into."

"When did you see them last?"

"Well, Larry Gene come by several times yesterday
afternoon, looking for Mickey. You see, Mickey lives with
me. Larry Gene's divorced from his first wife, Mickey's
mother. He's married again and has two children by his second
marriage. But they don't have the room or the money to take
care of Mickey, too. Mickey's mother is remarried and lives
over in Glasgow in Kentucky. His brother lives with them.
Mickey visits them some, but he'd druther live here with me.
I'm real glad to have him here. He's a sweet boy. He's got a job
at school and does his share to help with our living expenses. I
just get a small pension, you see, so money's pretty tight.

"Anyway, Larry Gene kept driving by in his truck yesterday
afternoon, and finally Mickey come home from school, and
he went over and got in his daddy's truck. Mickey's cousin
Kenny lives a few houses down from here. He was in the truck
with them, too."

Inez Thaxton paused to take a pinch of snuff from a small
box in her lap and tuck it under her lip. Then she continued,

"Me and Shirley-she's Larry's second wife-was 'settin' out
there in the yard. Larry and the boys pulled up in front of
the house in the truck. We went out to the truck. I said I had
to go to Nashville the next day and Larry Gene leaned out
and said, 'Mama, you can have my truck to go to Nashville
in the morning.' I said, 'Gordy and them is gonna take me.'
And he said, 'Well, you know you can have it.' And I said, 'I
know that I can.' And then he said, 'Mickey and Kenny will
be back in about 15 minutes,' but then he said, 'I will be in
jail.' That is what he said. So when I asked him why, he said,
'Well, ain't nobody gonna do me that way.' And then when

he started to leave, he looked around at me and he said, 'Bye, Mama. I love you. Make Shirley stay with you.' Then he said something kind of strange, though I didn't think much about it at the time. Larry Gene was always kidding around, and he was acting like he'd had a little too much to drink. He said, 'I may be back in an hour or two, and I may be back in a day or two, and I may be back in a week or two, and I may be back in three months.' That's the last thing he said.

"And I said, 'Mickey, don't you go off and stay off long, for you have to get back and get up in the morning and go to school.' And he said, 'Well, Nanny, I ain't a goin' to be gone long.' So that was the last word he said to me. And Kenny never said nothing. Then they just drove off.

"This morning, I went over to Nashville to take care of some business, and when I come back, they still hadn't shown up. I know something is terribly wrong."

"What do you think Larry meant when he said he might be back in a day or two or a week or two or in three months? Had he said anything before about going on a trip?"

Inez Thaxton shook her head. "He was talkin' kinda crazy, but I didn't think that much about it at the time. I could see he'd been drinking."

"Do you think they're in some .kind of trouble?"

"Yes,I do." ˙ -

"Maybe they drove somewhere and had car trouble."

"Oh, we'd have heard by now. They'd have got word back somehow."

"Do you think any of Larry Gene's or the boys' friends might have known where they went?" Inez was silent for a moment, searching her memory. "I don't know. Well, come to think of it, Larry Gene did say something to Mickey a few days ago about a friend of Mickey's, Curt Fishburn. He and

Curt had gone somewhere together. I could tell Larry Gene didn't want me to hear what they were talking about. He and Mickey moved off where I couldn't hear them, but they had their heads together and Larry Gene was laughing the way he does when he's been up to something."

"Do you know where I could find this Curt Fishburn?"

"My daughter, Polly Summers, would know. Her boy Kenny and Curt Fishburn were in school together."

"Kenny is the other boy who is missing, right?"

"Yes.

"I'd like to talk to Kenny's parents anyway. You said they live on Galen Road?"

"Yes. It's just over yonder." She arose from the couch with some effort, went to the screen door, and pointed out the road where Kenny lived. "Kenny's mother is my daughter, Pauline. We all call her Polly. She's Larry Gene's sister. Her husband, Kenny's father, is Carl Douglas Summers."

"Do you have pictures of Mickey and his father?" "Yes, I do." She took some snapshots out of an album and handed them to Jake.

"One other thing, can you describe the truck they were in?"

"It's painted yellow. Larry said it has four-wheel drive. I think it's a Chevrolet." Jake thanked her and left.

The Summers home where Kenny lived was within a couple of miles on Galen Road, at the bottom of a hill.

Old cars, some needing minor work, some needing major work, and some just plain junk were lined up just to the left of the house. A dirt and gravel driveway, badly needing scraping, separated the house from the row of old cars. A small house trailer sat at the end of the driveway. It served as a storage area for tools and a place to sleep if one of the Summers boys got caught up in a job and didn't want to come to the house. The

Summers house was a frame structure with a front porch and steps that looked as if they were made from rough lumber and never painted. The house was big and rambling. It showed the family's lack of wealth. The furniture was old, and for the most part, needed replacing. Nothing was thrown away until it was totally useless. Because of the size of the family, every bit of spare room was used as a sleeping area for someone. Kenny had shared a room with another brother on the second floor. Like her mother, Polly kept her house neat and orderly in spite of such a large family.

When Jake knocked, a woman who looked like a replica of Inez Thaxton twenty years younger, came to the door.

"Mrs. Summers?"

"Yes."

"My name is Jake Nixon. I'm a reporter from the newspaper. I wonder if I could ask you a few questions about your missing son?"

She was every bit as agitated as her mother. Her eyes were red from crying. She was quite willing to talk to Jake. She held a damp, balled-up handkerchief in one hand and dabbed at her eyes with it from time to time.

"Kenny wouldn't stay away from home all night unless he told me he was spending the night with somebody," she told the reporter. "He just wouldn't do that. He would either come and tell me his self or he would tell one of his brothers or whatever. When he didn't come home for supper last night, I got really worried. By this morning, when he still hadn't come home, the whole family got upset. We kept hoping that maybe they'd had a flat tire or something like that and couldn't get home. But when they still hadn't showed up by noon, I went to the sheriff's department and reported him missing."

"What did they tell you?"

"They said he hadn't been gone long enough to make it an official missing person case. They said not to worry, that Kenny would probably be home soon, but they would ask around if anyone had seen him and Mickey."

At that point, she broke down and wept. The sight of a parent weeping for a missing child awoke an old, wrenching hurt inside Jake. He thought about the night his own son hadn't come home. Later that night, the police had come and told him that his boy had been killed. It had been many years ago. It didn't get any easier. He thought that a parent never recovered from that kind of loss.

His heart filled with sympathy for this woman.

He waited with his own hurting memories, until she had regained control. Then he asked for a picture of Kenny, which Polly Summers gave him.

Jake said, "Your mother mentioned a friend of Mickey'S, Curt Fishburn. She said Larry Gene had been running around with Curt a few days ago. It is possible Curt might have some idea where they could have gone. Do you know Fishburn?"

"Yes, I know Curt. He and Kenny were in school together at one time although Curt's a couple of years or so older than Kenny and Mickey."

"What can you tell me about him?"

"Well, what do you want to know?"

"At this point, I'm not really sure. He seems to be the only possible lead as to where Larry Gene and the boys might be."

"Curt was hurt in a hunting accident a few years ago. He was accidentally shot. He's been partially disabled since then. His wife works. She has a daughter by a previous marriage who lives with them. I guess it's possible that Curt was running around with Larry Gene. Most of Mickey's friends know Larry Gene and like him. He's that kind of guy. I don't think Larry Gene ever completely grew up."

She told Jake how he could find where Curt Fishburn lived. "We sure would appreciate anything you could do to help us find those boys and their father, Mr. Nixon," she said, again on the verge of tears.

"Well, I can't promise anything, Mrs. Summers. It's really up to the sheriff's department to find them if they actually are missing. I just thought I'd ask around a bit to see what I could turn up. Let's hope they come back sometime today with a simple explanation about where they've been."

"I'm prayin' real hard for that," she said, but her expression was doubtful.

Jake's next stop was the sheriff's department, where he talked to a deputy friend who was familiar with the case.

"Oh, heck, I reckon they're going to turn up," the deputy told him. "Jake, you got to realize, Larry Gene Jones is an irresponsible guy who's always getting into some kind of mischief. He's been in and out of jail several times. If you want my opinion, he got himself and those boys in some kind of scrape and they're off hiding until things cool off. Give 'em a day or two and they'll be back."

"I hope you're right," Jake said, but his reporter's instinct told him it wasn't going to be that simple. He was becoming increasingly interested in the case. He had a premonition that he was on the trail of a story that was going to involve a lot more than a missing man and a couple of teenage boys.

Jake then hunted up Mickey's friend, Curt Fishburn. He found him at home, watching television. At first, Fishburn was not as willing to talk about the matter as Mickey's grandmother and aunt. He appeared uncomfortable and uneasy.

Jake persisted. "You're a good friend of the boys and Larry Gene. Do you think they've gotten in some kind of trouble?"

Curt shrugged, avoiding Jake's eyes. "Anything's possible with Larry Gene."

"According to Mickey's grandmother, you and Larry Gene were running around together some this past week. Did he say anything that would give you some idea where they might have gone yesterday?"

Curt chewed at his lip. He shifted uncomfortably in his chair, glancing at Jake, then away. He looked down at jeans, picking at them nervously. "I might know something, but I don't want to talk about it if you're going to print it in the newspaper. I don't want to get mixed up in one of Larry Gene's messes."

"Okay. This is off the record. I promise. I won't use anything you tell me in a newspaper story. I'd just like to get some kind of lead on where they might have gone."

"Well, I don't know if this has anything at all to do with where they are. Last week, some friends of mine, Keith Rowe, his wife Teresa, and Larry Gene, come by my house. We sat around talking and had a few beers. Larry Gene said he wanted to drive down to Trousdale County to see about a marijuana patch he'd heard about. Real good, top-grade stuff, he'd heard. So after a while, we got in his truck and drove down there. Larry Gene and I got out of the truck near a pond and went over into the property. We did get a look at that marijuana Larry Gene was talking about. It was being grown behind a big, high wall alongside a tobacco barn. Larry Gene was real interested in that marijuana. I think he might have tried to crawl over the wall, but the wife of the fellow that owns the property saw us and run us off."

"How'd she run you off?"

"She yelled at us and fired off a shotgun over our heads. Me 'n Larry Gene took off running. We got off that place.

But I heard this morning that Larry Gene and Mick and Kenny had gone off somewhere yesterday and hadn't come back, I got to thinking about that marijuana patch. I've been sitting here wondering if Larry Gene got it in his head to go back over there."

"Do you know whose property that marijuana was on?"

"It's a farm belonging to a fellow named Jerry Ward."

"Where is the farm located?"

"On farm road 141 a few miles south of Hartsville. Across the river."

"How do you reckon Larry Gene heard about this marijuana?" "Heck, I don't know. Teresa, Keith's wife, might have told him. She's Jerry Ward's first cousin. I don't think it's no great secret, though. There's a lot of marijuana being grown in Trousdale County. I think folks around there pretty well know where it is."

Jake thanked him and returned to the newspaper office. He reported what he had found out to the city editor, leaving out for the time being his interview with Curt Fishburn. "I don't think we have a story at this point. There's still a pretty good chance the man and those two boys will turn up."

"Okay. Keep in touch with the situation. If it turns into an official missing person's case, we'll run something. Did you get some pictures?"

Jake nodded. He showed Bevans the pictures of the two teenage boys. "They're not real great. Just snapshots. It's the best I could do."

"Well, they're better than nothing. If we get word from the sheriff's department that they're on the missing person's list, we'll run the pictures in a box on the front page." Bevans turned to face his computer.

Jake started to leave the office, but paused at the door. "If they really are missing, I may want to run down to Trousdale County."

Bevans swung his chair back around. He looked at Jake sharply. "You're not telling me everything."

"At this point, I don't know if I have anything to tell. Let's wait until tomorrow."

"Just be careful if you go nosing around Trousdale County. The natives over there are not very friendly to outsiders, especially to someone from Macon County."

"I know. I grew up in Trousdale County."

Jake went to his desk. He sat there for a while, staring off into space. Something Curt Fishburn had said was echoing in his mind. *There's a lot of marijuana being grown in Trousdale County. I think folks around there pretty well know where it is. "*

Once again, Jake Nixon experienced the kind of inner tingle he felt when he sensed he was stumbling into a very big story.

Chapter 4

September 5, 1985

Polly Summers later said, "That whole day, September 4, went by. No Kenny. I called Inez. She said Larry and Mickey hadn't come home. Kenny's brothers and his father were getting real worried too. Kenny didn't show up that night. By then he'd been gone the night of September 3, all the next day, and the night of September the 4. I was about out of my mind with worry. I had this terrible, cold feeling inside that something awful bad had happened to him.

"I went back to the sheriff's department the next day that was Thursday, September 5, and told them, 'Look here, my boy has been missing for two days and two nights, ever since Tuesday. You've just got to do something.' So they said then that they would make it official. They put out a • nationwide bulletin on Kenny with his description and a description of who he was with and a description of the kind of truck they were in."

Jake Nixon got word shortly after lunch that the sheriff's department had officially listed Larry Gene Jones and the two boys as missing persons.

"We can go with this story now," he told his editor, handing him the computer disk containing his write-up of his interviews with Inez Thaxton and Polly Summers the day before.

"Okay. We'll use it in a box on the front page with those pictures of the missing boys. Maybe we'll get lucky and somebody will remember seeing them."

"I think I'll spend the afternoon in Trousdale County." His editor gave him a quizzical look. "You were very mysterious about that yesterday. Have you got some kind of lead?"

"Maybe. It's pretty slim. One of Mickey's friends, a fellow named Curt Fishburn, rode down to a farm in Trousdale County last week with Larry Gene Jones. Apparently, Larry Gene got it in his head to raid a marijuana patch on a farm owned bya fellow named Jerry Ward. Some woman, probably Jerry's wife, ran them off with a shotgun. Could be Larry Gene decided to nose around down there again."

"It's slim, but worth looking into," Bevans agreed.

Jake went on. "According to what Fishburn said, there's marijuana being grown in farms all over the county. That brings up some interesting questions. If it's true, then the stuff is being grown right under the noses of the local authorities. Don't they know it's there? If they do, why aren't they doing anything about it? Could be this is developing into a bigger story than just the missing fellows."

The city editor gave him a thoughtful look. "Jake, you're a heck of a good investigative reporter. I can see you've got your radar working overtime. You're right, it could be a big story, but you could also find yourself in a very sticky situation, poking around something like that. You could turn up mysteriously missing like the Jones fellow and the two boys."

Jake shrugged. Personal danger was not something that concerned him a great deal any longer. "What has me baffled is what happened to them. Three fellows and a big, yellow truck don't just vanish off the face of the earth."

"Well, for right now, that's the big story. Concentrate on that."

"Gotcha, boss."

Jake left the office. He gazed for a moment at his car, baking in the sun in the parking lot. He sighed. Maybe next week he'd see about getting the air conditioner fixed. On the way out of town, he stopped to have a brief talk with the sheriff. Sheriff Mercer was a man of medium build, about five five, but stumpy and heavyset. He was about fifty, had thin, dark brown hair, and wore glasses. Jake had never seen the sheriff without a plug of tobacco tucked in his cheek.

The sheriff had no new information to give Jake. He said that Polly Summers had been to see him. He had a boy about Kenny's age so he could sympathize wholeheartedly with how worried she was. He said he was going to do everything he could to find Larry Gene and the missing boys, although he hadn't the slightest clue as to where they might have gone or what could have happened to them. It was a twenty-minute drive. Jake rolled down all the windows in his car. It didn't help much. The wind that blew in was hot and dusty. Jake felt his shirt sticking to his back.

He arrived at Hartsville, drove slowly through the small town, then south on farm road 141. When he passed a field where some tobacco cutters were working, he pulled to the shoulder of the road and stopped. He got out and walked over to the fence.

"Hi," he said.

The cutter nearest the road drew his forearm across his perspiring forehead and nodded.

"Hot day."

"You got that right."

The cutter moved over to the fence .Jake offered him a cigarette.

"Thanks."

Jake lit one for himself. Then he asked, "Wonder if you could tell me where Jerry Ward's farm is located."

"Sure. It's just down the road a piece. On your right. You'll see some buildings, a barn, a trailer house, and a bunch of chicken coops. Jerry raises chickens."

"Thanks. The Ward family is well-known, but I couldn't remember where Jerry's farm is located. I grew up here in Trousdale County."

"That a fact?"

"Yeah. My dad had a small farm not far from here. I went to school up to the fifth grade in Hartsville. My name's Jake Nixon."

"Pleased to meet you, Mr. Nixon. I'm Ricky Claridy."

They shook hands. Ricky was obviously the friendly, talkative type who welcomed the excuse to take a break. Jake asked, "Have you lived around here long, Ricky?"

"All my life. Twenty-two years."

"I guess you know a lot of people around here. Do you know Jerry Ward, Ricky?"

"Oh, sure. Everybody around here knows Jerry and his family."

"Would you happen to know Larry Gene Jones from Lafayette?

Claridy gave him a peculiar look. "Yeah, I know Larry. Why are you asking?"

"Did you know that Larry Gene and his boy, Mickey, and his nephew Kenny Summers are missing?"

The tobacco cutter looked startled. "Missing? What do you mean, missing?"

"They drove off from Lafayette Tuesday afternoon. Today's Thursday. Nobody's seen them since they left on Tuesday. The police have them on a nationwide missing persons list."

"My God," Claridy muttered, shaking his head.

"Do you know what kind of truck Larry Jones drives?"

"Yeah, a yellow Chevy four-by-four."

"Have you by any chance seen it around here?"

"Not in the last few days."

"Then you have seen Larry Jones in his truck before Tuesday?"

Ricky Claridy was beginning to look at Nixon suspiciously. "Are you with the law, mister?"

"No, Ricky. I work on a newspaper in Macon County. I'm a reporter. I talked to Mickey's grandmother and Kenny's mother yesterday. Those poor people are just about out of their minds with worry. All I'm interested in is to try and do what I can to help that family find those missing boys. If you know anything that would help, I'd sure appreciate it if you'd tell me."

Rickey looked uncomfortable. "I might know a few things, but it sure would get me in trouble if it got in the newspaper."

"I won't print anything you don't want me to."

"You sure about that?"

"Give you my word. All I want to do is find Larry Jones and those two boys. That's the only story I'm after. I'll tell you what I've found out so far, I've talked to a friend of Mickey's, Curt Fishburn. He said he and Mickey's daddy were around here last week. He said they snuck onto Jerry Ward's property looking for some marijuana they thought was planted there."

Ricky Claridy nodded soberly. "Yeah, I know about that. We were cutting tobacco around here last week, me and Johnny Rose and Johnny Reed, so we were driving up and down 141 quite a bit. We saw Larry Gene and Curt Fishburn walking along the shoulder of the road a short ways from the Ward farm. We stopped to give them a ride. I remember they were both sweating. Larry Gene said they'd been running through the brush. He laughed about it, like it was a big joke. We took them up the road a ways' to where Larry's truck was parked."

"Curt Fishburn said they came over with Keith Roe and his wife."

"Yeah; they was in Larry's truck, waiting."

"D'you think Curt was telling me the truth about the marijuana on Jerry Ward's farm?"

Ricky grinned slyly. He glanced around as if to make sure no one overheard him, then said in a low voice, *"Oh,* there's some over there, all right. Top-grade stuff. We was working almost directly across the street from the Ward farm about a week ago. We went over there to get a drink of water. Soon as I got on the property, I smelled it. Smells like a skunk. Some people call it skunk weed."

"Curt told me it was being grown behind some kind of high fence near the barn." Ricky nodded. "More like a high wall than a fence." Then he looked at Jake with a curious expression. "You think that has anything to do with Larry Gene and the boys being missing?"

"Well, I don't know. From what Curt said, Larry Gene was very interested in that patch of marijuana. I thought I'd drive down here and nose around a bit. Of course, I may be way off base. I don't even know that they came down to Trousdale County on Tuesday. You say you didn't see Larry's truck on 141 that day."

"No, but we was doing some cutting on a field some distance away from here on Tuesday, so I wouldn't have seen them if they was around here."

"Are there other places around here they might have gone looking for marijuana?"

Ricky laughed. "Mister, there's marijuana patches in farms all over this county."

Jake nodded thoughtfully. "That's what Curt said. Well, thanks, Ricky. I'd better be moving along."

"I sure hope you find out where they've gone. Mickey and Kenny are real nice boys. I can see why their folks would be worried."

Jake nodded. He walked back to his car, started the engine, and drove a short distance until he saw the chicken coops and barn Ricky had described.

He slowly pulled into the driveway of the Ward property. He didn't know what he expected to find. He wasn't sure what he'd say to Jerry Ward.

He stopped his car in the yard and got out. There was a house and a mobile home on the property. Behind the house were the chicken coops and the barn that both Curt

Fishburn and Ricky Claridy had described.

The place looked deserted.

Jake walked slowly around the house. He could hear the sound of hammering coming from the vicinity of the barn. The field on the other side of a wire fence was grown up with tall weeds. It all looked peaceful and quiet. He couldn't even smell the odor of skunk weed that Ricky Claridy had described.

Jake shook his head. This was beginning to look like a wild goose chase. Then he saw a tall, husky man walking toward him from the barn.

When Jake returned to the newspaper office ,he reported what happened to his editor. "I couldn't find anyone who saw Jones or the boys in Trousdale County on Tuesday. I did talk to a tobacco cutter who confirmed Curt Fishburn's story about Curt and Larry Jones sneaking on the Ward property last week. Then I stopped by Jerry Ward's farm. Jerry Ward came out to talk to me. He told me he didn't know anything about Larry Gene Jones and the two boys and hadn't seen them. I don't know if he's telling the truth or not, but there was no yellow truck anywhere to be seen, and certainly no place to hide one that I could see.

"If Larry Gene and the boys had come. over here on Tuesday, they vanished into thin air."

Chapter 5

Later ...September 5

In September of 1985, Charles Robinson had been sheriff of Trousdale County for twelve years. He was a big man, six feet two, weighing 210 pounds. He was in his mid-50s with sandy hair. The thing most noticed about him was his booming voice. When Charles Robinson spoke, he was given attention.

On the morning of September 4, while at the jail in Hartsville, Sheriff Robinson received a phone call from the Macon County sheriff advising him that three people had left Macon County the day before and had not returned home.

When told the names of the three missing persons, Robinson immediately recognized the name "Larry Jones." He knew of Jones' prison record. He'd had Larry Jones in his prison at Hartsville in the past. Considering Larry's talent for getting into trouble, Sheriff Robinson suspected this could be a serious matter. He immediately began interrogating people in the area who might have some information about Larry Jones' recent activities.

Friday, September 6

About two o'clock in the afternoon, on Friday, September 6, Philip Bay, a farmer in nearby Wilson County, was driving along Mitchell Road in the direction of highway 141. Mitchell Road went through two small towns, Providence and Bellwood, in Wilson County. It was a narrow country road, seldom traveled. Bay was approaching the Trousdale-Wilson county line.

Suddenly, he put on his brakes. In the road, partially

blocking his path, was a yellow pickup truck. Bay got out and approached the truck. He first thought the driver must have had engine trouble and left the truck while he went for help.

Then Bay saw something that sent a chill up his spine. The truck was riddled with bullet holes. Bay got back to his car in a hurry. At the first telephone he could find, he reported the abandoned vehicle to the Wilson County sheriff's department. "You'd better get somebody out here right away," he said urgently. "Somebody's shot the hell out of that truck."

Now the law enforcement agencies of three adjoining counties, Macon, Trousdale, and Wilson, were directly involved in the missing persons case.

Deputy Sheriff Ray Webber was the first Wilson County law official check on the truck. He found that the abandoned vehicle was a Chevrolet four-wheel drive pickup.

Webber noted several items in the truck. On the seat was a partially empty bottle of whisky. On the floorboard was a beer can and there were several other beer cans in the bed of the truck as well as spent shells and pieces of what looked like weeds or grass.

Webber towed the truck into Lebanon, the county seat of Wilson County.

Saturday, September 7

Jake Nixon received word that the missing truck had been found. He got busy on the phone, putting in calls to the sheriff's department in Wilson and Trousdale Counties and to the Tennessee Bureau of Investigation (TBI). He got the following statement from a criminalist supervisor with the TBI:

"We received a call from Terry Ashe, the sheriff of Wilson County, where an abandoned truck had been found on a road in the outlying area of northern Wilson County. Sheriff Ashe asked if we could send some people to look at this truck, that it appeared to have been shot up, to see what evidence we could find. We proceeded to Wilson County, to Lebanon, to the sheriff's office where they took us to Ray Webber's tow-in lot where we viewed the truck. We determined at that time it would be best to view this truck at the crime lab where we had facilities to raise the truck and look for evidence."

William J. Haney Jr., forensic chemist with the State of Tennessee crime laboratory, said he performed tests on the weeds found in the truck. "I took a random representative sample from each of the items, checked it under the microscope and performed a chemical color test on it. As a result of my test, I identified the material. In each case it was identified as marijuana."

On September 9, Franklin Evetts, agent with the TBI, was assigned to the case of the missing men. Evetts was a man in his mid-60s. His hair was white, his height and build medium. He dressed casually and wore glasses. He had an arrogant manner and speech. He had been a TBI agent for eighteen years. His assignment now: find Larry Jones and the two missing boys.

Evetts spent his time driving between Lafayette, Hartsville and his home in Lebanon. He was working closely with Sheriff Mercer of Macon County and Sheriff Robinson of Trousdale County. They checked on rumors in Lafayette that the missing man and boys had gone on a marijuana patch raid. They interviewed friends of the trio and tobacco cutters who had been topping burley tobacco in Trousdale County in late summer. Eventually, their questioning led them to cutters who had worked in fields across the road from the Ward farm.

Chapter 6

Monday, September 9

Jake Nixon's reporter's intuition had been correct. The missing persons case had become front page materiaL ow that the missing truck had been found, there were stories about the case in newspapers every day.

A week had passed with no hint of what had become of Jones and the two boys. That they had been involved in some kind of shoot-out was obvious from the condition of the truck. That marijuana was involved had also been established. Beyond that, there was no clue about whether the missing trio was dead or alive or where they might be.

The area in Wilson County where the truck had been found was thoroughly searched. The fields adjoining the road were combed. Nothing was found. Had the shooting occurred at the site where the truck was located? Had it occurred somewhere else and the truck driven here? When the truck was examined, it was found that the gears were locked in a way that the truck could not be driven. Then how did it get to the deserted road in Wilson County?

These were some of the puzzling questions that were spawning a flood of rumors. The strange disappearance of the three persons was the topic of conversation and conjecture in cafes, on street corners, in private homes. The story was aired on TV evening newscasts. It was beginning to draw statewide attention.

It was keeping Jake Nixon busy. Early in the week, he again paid a visit to Kenny Summers' family where he again interviewed Polly Summers.

"We're getting all kinds of phone calls," Kenny's mother

said tearfully. "People will call and say they thought they saw Kenny or Mickey someplace, but nothing has come of it. We heard about the truck being found before the law let us know. Some people we know that was connected with the police department found out about the truck this weekend and come over and told us.

"One of Kenny's brothers went to Lebanon, but they told him he couldn't see the truck right then. They did tell him what kind of shape it was in. They said the truck had been shot up real bad. They said when it was found it had flat tires and one of the doors was open. There was a small amount of blood on it. It had a bloody handprint on one of the doors.

"A couple of Kenny's brothers drove down to where they'd found the truck and just drove around in that area thinking maybe Kenny and them was hiding somewhere and they would come out."

Jake asked, "How many brothers and sisters does Kenny .have?"

"Five brothers-Wayne, Carl Allen, Richard, Tommy, and Jason. His sister is Patricia."

She went on. "The sheriff's department told us that people might talk to us where they wouldn't talk to them, you know. So we've been doin' a lot of footwork, and anything we find out, we go back and tell the sheriff. If somebody called to say they seen them goin' somewhere, we'd go right out there to try and chase them down. Like, somebody called and said that they seen Kenny in town late Thursday night. They said he was in a black car. From then on, his brothers have stayed out on the road every night, just drivin' around in case they did run into him. Well, sure enough, Sunday night, they saw a black car fittin' the description of the one that Kenny was supposed to have been in, and they chased that car home. It went into a trailer park. They went up to the trailer and knocked on the door. The people there didn't know Kenny. They didn't know anything about Kenny. The boys were so disappointed."

At that point, Kenny's mother broke down. Jake was painfully aware of the tension the family was under. He knew they were going through hell, not knowing where their son was, hoping he was alive somewhere, but filled with dread that he was dead.

When Polly regained her composure, she said, "The sheriff here in Macon County has been real nice. He's more than just a sheriff. He's a friend. He's tried to comfort us. He's tried to tell us that Kenny and Mickey might have to.okit in their heads to run off somewhere. Teenage boys sometimes do things like that, he said. Maybe they got in some trouble about marijuana. You know they found traces of marijuana in the truck. So maybe Kenny and Mickey knew they were in trouble about that, and they're just afraid to come home. I kept telling them that Kenny took a bath every day. He had to brush his teeth. He had to wash his hair. Kenny had to have clean clothes every day, and I kept telling them that he would not stay gone that long without being able to do all of that. If we could just find them...just know for sure what happened, maybe it wouldn't be so hard for us."

As he talked to the family, Jake learned that from early on, Kenny's family had a feeling that the disappearance might be linked to the Ward family. They knew that Larry Gene had been nosing around the marijuana patch on the Ward farm a week before the disappearance.

As early as September 4, the morning after the disappearance, Gordy Thaxton, Larry Gene's half brother, and Kenny's brother, Wayne, had driven by the Ward farm, wondering if they might see Larry Gene's yellow truck or some signs of the missing boys. However, like Jake when he'd driven to the Ward farm later that same day, they had seen nothing.

They had met a stone wall when they asked questions of neighbors of the Wards. People in Trousdale County tended to be closemouthed when asked any questions about the Ward family. And there was another factor. The people who lived in Trousdale County exhibited resentment and suspicion of anyone from Macon County. This territorial instinct put the Ward's neighbors on their side against the outsiders they considered intruders.

Jake thought he had been lucky to have encountered the tobacco cutter, Ricky Claridy, the first day he went over there. Others in the area wouldn't have been so friendly. .

Back at the newspaper, Jake and his editor discussed the case over cups of coffee. Jake said, "I've been in touch with Sheriff Robinson in Trousdale County and Sheriff Terry Ashe in Wilson County: I've also talked with the TBI agent, Franklin Evetts. They don't have any positive leads at this point. The only thing they feel pretty certain about is that marijuana was somehow involved in the shooting because of the traces found in the truck."

"You've been as close to this thing as anybody. What do you think?" his editor asked.

Jake sipped his coffee thoughtfully, then shook his head. "I'm as baffled as the rest of them. I keep thinking Jerry Ward's family is somehow involved. Both Curt Fishburn and Ricky Claridy, the tobacco cutter, insist Ward is raising marijuana on his place. Real top-grade stuff, they tell me. If it's true, the street value could be worth several hundred thousand dollars. We're talking big-time drug dealing here. Maybe Jones and the boys were sneaking around the Ward property that day.

Maybe there was some shooting, and they drove off in a hurry and abandoned the truck on that deserted dirt road in Wilson County. Maybe they're hiding out somewhere, afraid of the Wards or the law.

"On the other hand," Jake continued, "I've driven by the Ward farm a couple of times this past week. I even talked with Jerry Ward. I can't find any witnesses that saw Jones and the boys near .the Ward farm that day. I can't even be sure about the marijuana. The first time I went over there, the field around the barn was head-high in weeds. But since then, Ward has cleaned up the place, bushhogged all .the weeds down. There is a high fence, almost like a wall around an area next to the barn, the way Fishburn and Claridy described it, but I couldn't get close enough to see if there was any marijuana behind the fence. Claridy claimed you could smell it. I didn't smell anything."

"Maybe they didn't go to the Ward farm at all. You've been told there are marijuana patches in other farms in Trousdale County."

Jake nodded. "That's sure a possibility. Especially since the truck was found so far away from the Ward farm." He put his empty cup on the editor's desk. "Well, the next thing I'm going to do is drive up to Glasgow. I want to interview Mickey's mother, Sherry Grimsley, for another human interest angle. Maybe she can add something we've overlooked."

Glasgow, Kentucky, was a short distance across the Kentucky border. Jake talked with friends of Sherry Grimsley at the nursing home where she worked. He was told that grief and worry over her missing son was pushing her near an emotional breakdown.

He called Sherry Grimsley and she agreed to an interview. Jake found Sherry Grimsley to be an attractive woman thirty- six years of age. She was 5'2" and weighed about 120 pounds. The strain she was under was obvious to Jake. She was pale. Her eyes were red and swollen from crying and lack of sleep. Her hands were trembling. It was clear that she was a woman at the breaking point.

She told Jake, "The last time I seen Mickey, he was standing right there. He was laughing and talking. He'd spent the weekend with us, and was going back to Lafayette to start school. Mickey needed some lunch money. I had a ten dollar bill. That was all I had here at the house, and I gave him that. The night he disappeared, the third of September, around eleven 0'clock, I got a terrible feeling that something bad was happening. I said, 'Lord, something is gonna happen. I have the awfulest dread on my mind. It's just like I know something is gonna happen, something bad, but I don't know what it is....'"

Jake said, "I've talked to Mickey's grandmother and to Kenny's family. They seem to think the Ward family down in Trousdale County might have something to do with the boys' disappearance. Larry Jones had sneaked on the Ward property the week before, trying to get his hands on some marijuana they claim is being grown there."

Sherry Grimsley nodded. "I heard about that. It sounds like the kind of darn fool thing Larry would do. Did they tell you one of the Wards drove up in a van to Inez's house the night the boys disappeared?"

Jake looked at her with surprise. This was a bit of information that was new to him. "They didn't tell me about that."

"Well, Polly and Inez-all of them-are so upset, they don't know what they're saying half the time. All I can tell you is what Inez and Shirley told me. Inez said this van drove up in front of her house. She went out on the porch. Before she could talk to the driver, he drove off. That was sometime on the night of September 3. Then, the van drove up in front of Polly's house and Larry's and Shirley's house. Shirley said she recognized the driver. She claims it was Jerry Ward."

"Did he tell them what he wanted?" She shook her head. "If it was Jerry Ward, we don't know why he was driving around their houses. Maybe he wanted to tell them something but changed his mind."

"When I talked with Polly earlier today, she said the sheriff suggested the boys might have got in trouble over the marijuana and have run off for a while."

Sherry nodded. "We've thought Larry might have taken the boys to either Indiana or Florida. He has friends in both states that he could stay with. We've contacted Major Clifton Duncan, a local detective, to look into that. So far, he hasn't been able to find anything. Monday night Inez called to tell me that they had found the truck. I've been told that they've searched all around where the truck was found. I've heard they even had bloodhounds and heli-. copters to search the area. I think they're talking about dragging the river, but I don't know if they've done that yet."

Jake said, "The location has everyone puzzled. It's miles from the Ward farm. Do you have any idea what they might have been doing in that part of Wilson County?" She shook her head. She hesitated for a moment, then asked, "Have you ever heard of a man named Carl Shoopman?"

Jake thought for a moment. "The name is familiar, Isn't he some kind of psychic? I seem to remember that the police have used him on some occasions."

"Yes, that's him. Carl Shoopman has helped people in this area with various problems. He's supposed to be especially good at finding things-or people-that are missing. My husband thinks we should get him to help us. Lord knows, the police haven't been able to find a trace of those boys. I'm ready to try almost anything.

"My husband told me about Carl. He had heard about him some time ago through friends where he works at the RR Donnelly plant. I had heard of him, but I didn't know anything about him. Anyway, my husband asked if I would call him, so I did. He was 'real nice. He's agreed to go with the sheriff and the TBI man around the area to see if he has any feeling about where the boys might be." Jake thought that this case was becoming more bizarre with each passing day. Now a psychic had been called in to try and solve a mystery that had local and state police stumped.

Jake Nixon had never quite made up his mind about psychics. He'd covered stories about them before. He'd seen them working with police on missing persons cases. Sometimes they produced remarkable results, sometimes they didn't. Jake was something of a skeptic about psychic phenomena, as he was about most things he couldn't see or touch, but he tried to keep an open mind on the subject.

Jake decided to interview Carl Shoopman. For years afterward, every time he thought about Carl Shoopman and the part Shoopman played in the case of the missing men from Macon County, Jake would feel the hair on the back of his neck prickle. He couldn't explain what happened. It was something beyond the ordinary experiences of the physical world. Shoopman somehow caught a glimpse of things that the law enforcement agencies with all their sophisticated, scientific equipment couldn't see.

Jake knew that Carl Shoopman had acquired a considerable reputation in the area for an unexplained ability to find missing objects and people. Shoopman was so well-known in the area and so besieged by people asking for help from his psychic abilities that he sometimes had to slip away on weekends on fishing trips to have some privacy. Jake called Shoopman and set up an appointment for an interview.

Shoopman lived with his elderly mother and his son in a modest stone house a short distance from a freeway bypass. The house was on a small lot with houses on either side. The yard was clean and neat. There were a few wellplaced flowers to add a touch of color. Behind the house was stacked cordwood used for winter heating. In the driveway was Shoopman's old green pickup truck.

Nixon found Shoopman to be a man in his forties. He was scarecrow thin to the point of emaciation. His complexion was sallow, his cheeks sunken. He did not look healthy. A ragged baseball cap covered his balding head constantly, whether he was indoors or out. The work clothes he wore indicated that here was a person who earned his living with hard work. Obviously, he was not cashing in on his recognized ability as a psychic.

Nixon saw in Carl's face a man who had not been given an easy road by life.

Looking at the modest surroundings in Shoopman's home, Nixon could see that these were poor, hardworking, down-to-earth people. The furniture was basic and worn. The one touch of extravagance was a large console color TV in the living room.

The strongest thing about Carl Shoopman was his eyes. They seemed to burn with some kind of fierce inner energy that kept his frail body functioning.

The interview took place in Shoopman's kitchen. Shoopman spoke in the regional, colloquial manner indigenous to this rural area of Tennessee and Kentucky. The psychic began by telling Jake something about his childhood and the early discovery of his psychic powers. "As a child growing up," said Shoopman, "I was scared of the dark. I seen things all the time. People would call it ghosts now or spiritual beings. A lot of people don't believe in things like that, but I would see things, and I was immensely scared of the dark. I wouldn't even go outside by myself if I could help it. If I got very far from home, I would run until I got home, and I would see things, bad omens or bad letters. I could tell somebody if something bad was going to happen to them, down there in the area where I grew up. I ain't scared of the dark now, but I don't like to get out on a real dark night. I have cold chills running up and down me like vibrations.

"When I was a teenager, if I let myself go, I'd tell my mother things that were going to happen. Sometimes I even scared my own self the way these things would come true." "I like to have died several times when I was growing up. First, I almost died when I was a very young child from a bowel disease. Then I like to have died of tuberculosis when I was eight years old.

"I've been married and divorced twice. Had a son by my first wife. She neglected him. My mother has raised him since he was two years old. I got up my nerve and got married the second time. I have a daughter by my second marriage. My second wife left me for another man.

"A lot of people don't believe in what I call restless spirits. Some people call it ghosts or whatever. A lot of people don't believe in what they can't see with their own eyes. My own mother didn't believe in things like that. She'd say, 'Oh, you're just seeing things.' I told her I could see things nobody else could see.

"There's one I saw about two years ago right here in this house. It came one night when I stayed up late. It was raining cats and dogs and there was nobody here but me. My mother had gone somewhere and my son was away, too. I went to bed, and I was having one of those restless nights when I felt something was going to happen. Everything got real still. Then I heard the front door slam and footsteps, like a woman in high heels walking up through the hall. The room got real cold. I felt like I was in a freezer. In my mind, I thought, 'What's going on?' And then I saw a woman standing there at the foot of my bed. She had her hair done up in a bun at the back, the way women did many years ago. She wore a long dress and a white blouse like the style they had a long, long time ago. She wore a pin, a kind of brooch pin. And she was standing there, and she is a young-like woman. She was working her mouth, trying to tell me some thing or 'nother. I just froze solid. I was having cold chills. I wanted to cover my head up. I wanted to holler 'help.' But I couldn't move and my voice was froze. Then she just went away-went out through my door.

"The next day I told my mother about it. She said I was just seeing things, maybe dreaming. But I know better.

"A few nights later, a man carne to see me. It was raining cats and dogs again. Somebody had stolen a tractor from him and he come to see me and wanted to know if I could tell him anything about his stolen tractor. I described exactly how it happened. I told him two men got it. One man used to work for him. One watched while the other pushed it down past his house and drove it away. I said, 'You will get it back,' and I told him where to find it.

"Then I noticed that while I was talking this man kept looking around at the window. The man said, 'Did you see that woman standing out there in the rain, looking in the window?'

Then I knew it was the same woman I'd seen a couple of nights before at the foot of my bed."

Then Shoopman talked for a while about some of the missing persons cases he had worked on in which he had helped police in their search. He had been asked to help in other states as well as in local areas. "I like to study the unexplained things, like the Loch Ness monster, things like that," he said.

"A lot of people advertise that they can predict your future or tell you how to solve your problems. Most of those people are scams, out for money. If you're gifted the way I am, you are born with it. It's a gift. My door is open all the time to people who need help, and I do not charge for what I do. Therefore, I classify myself as more superior over these people that are good for a scam or try to do it for money. I've proved myself. It does my heart good if I can help my fellowman in any way, because I feel like that is what I was put on earth for."

Getting to the case of Larry Gene Jones and the two teenage boys, Shoopman said that Sherry, Joe Grimsley's wife, had called him several times about the missing trio. "I was working on another case when she first called," he explained. "I needed to get where I could concentrate on her son and the other two that were missing. My mind has to be working on a particular thing. I need to have a general description of what they look like, age, height, color of hair. Also their birth sign. I go a whole lot by a person's birth sign that tells me what character they are, and like that.

"Finally, about the third time Joe's wife called me-it was at nighttime-I told her they were not under water, I told her that the people involved were three men and a woman, and I thought Larry knew the woman. I said that they couldn't be found by air or by dragging. To find them you would have to walk right up to them. Now, I didn't tell her what I'm going to tell you, but I have a strong feeling that all three of them are dead."

It was Monday night, September 16. Mickey Jones, his father, and Kenny Summers had been missing for two weeks. Sherry Grimsley drove Carl Shoopman to Sheriff Ashe's office in Lebanon. With them were Sherry's daughter, Marsha, and a nephew, Jimmy Jackson. Jackson had been a deputy sheriff and a park ranger. Sherry explained to Sheriff Ashe that she had asked Carl Shoopman to help find the missing boys. Sheriff Ashe agreed to cooperate. Sherry waited in the office with her daughter while her nephew, Jimmy Jackson, along with a detective from the sheriff's office, and a TBI agent took Carl Shoopman on a drive in a sheriff's county patrol car around the area.

"If you want my opinion," the TBI agent said with an air of impatience, "we're wasting our time with this hocus pocus stuff."

"Sorry, sir, but I don't agree," the detective said. "I've worked with psychics before. Sometimes they can be very helpful. Mr. Shoopman has a reputation for being real good in missing persons cases."

First Shoopman asked to be driven down to the river that ran south of Hartsville. When they arrived at that area, Carl left the car and walked along the riverbank in deep thought. After a while, he returned to the car. He shook his head. "I just don't feel like they are in the river."

Then the officers took Shoopman around to several other areas, on some county roads he'd never been on before. On one of the roads, Carl suddenly got some strong feelings.

"Stop here!" he exclaimed. For a few minutes he sat in silence, overwhelmed by surging emotions.

"Something happened here," he said, nodding. "Something

drastic happened. It had something to do with shots fired. Two men were involved in this place. One of the men, I feel, was real mad. The other was more quiet like. He was a worker, a fellow who did hard work with his hands."

The detective and TBI agent exchanged surprised looks. This was the spot where the Jones truck had been found. After that, the TBI agent was less skeptical of Shoopman's ability.

Then they drove on several other country roads in the area, but Shoopman didn't pick up any more vibes. He said, "I have the feeling that they're in some kind of outbuilding or a barn ...buried in a barn."

"What direction do you think that would be from here?" the deputy asked. Shoopman concentrated on his inner feelings. "I think they're in the next county over."

"That would be Trousdale County."

"Well, that's the way we should go." Later, Carl Shoopman talked about that evening. "We drove over there and we came to a farm and I told them to stop the car. I got out of the car and walked over to the fence. In these cases, I go by my feelings. I had a real strong feeling there. I started feeling a tingling all over. It was like I'd grabbed a hold of an electric fence. I got to shaking from head to foot, the feelings were that strong.

''There was gunfire here!' I said. 'A lot of gunfire. See that old building over there?' I pointed to the area of the barn and shed. 'There's a clue there that would solve this case.' I had some real strong feelings about those outbuildings. I said, 'If you'd talk to those people that live there, I think they know a whole lot about what's happened to those three missing people.'" The place Shoopman was talking about was the Jerry Ward farm.

Chapter 7

While the search for Larry Jones and the two boys was reaching a climax, Howard Collins was in Alabama, working on a construction job for Bobby Ward. He couldn't keep his mind on his work. He couldn't sleep. His mind was constantly tormented with vivid memories of the events at Jerry Ward's farm on September 3.

That night, after Howard had tied up the boys and Larry Gene Jones and darkness had fallen- Jerry Ward's father, Hubert Jr., had ordered Howard to go get the company flatbed truck. He said they were going to use it to move the Jones truck out of the field. Howard walked up the hill to the house. He saw that the company truck had been moved since they drove it into the yard earlier that afternoon. He waited at the truck for a while, then Jerry Ward's father joined him.

With Hubert behind the wheel, they drove down to the field where the Jones truck had been left. Its motor had been running since Larry Gene Jones and the two boys had surrendered. Now Howard crawled under the truck with a flashlight in an attempt to find out why the gears would not mesh. He could not get the vehicle to operate. Hubert ordered him to connect a chain from the company truck to the Jones truck.

With Howard driving the company truck and Hubert behind the wheel of the Jones pickup, they pulled around to the shed beside the barn. There, on Hubert's orders, they unloaded from the pickup the marijuana that Larry Gene Jones and the boys had taken.

They stashed the marijuana in the shed and covered it with plywood and sheets of tin. Then they pulled the Jones truck across the road to the heavy utility trailer. They propped runners against the trailer and pushed the Jones truck backwards, up the runners onto the bed of the utility trailer.

While they were getting the 'truck on the trailer, there was occasional traffic on the road. Collins later testified, "There was several cars that passed by. At that time we would be as quiet as we could and try to be unseen."

As Hubert and Collins were struggling to get the Jones truck on the trailer, Jerry Ward came across the road and up the hill to join them. Collins later said, "He was very upset and using some pretty harsh words to his dad. He wanted to know what in the hell was taking so long and what in the hell was all the noise about. He wanted us to stop the noise. And he was demanding about that."

At last the Jones truck was on the trailer. The trailer was hooked to the company truck. They got in the truck and pulled out onto highway 141,headed in the general direction of Hartsville.

A little while earlier, as they were moving the truck out of the Ward farmyard, the headlights had flashed for a moment across the chicken yard. Howard saw the two teenage boys still kneeling there, their hands tied behind their backs. He said, "Just before I pulled the truck out of the field to cross the road and load it up, I cut the headlamps on. The boys were in the field beside the fence where the chicken coops are, still on their knees at that time."

It was the last time he saw them.

With the Jones truck on the flatbed trailer behind the company truck, Collins drove for several minutes north, on highway 141 in the direction of Hartsville, then turned off to the right. They drove on some back roads until Hubert Ward Jr. ordered Collins to stop. It was a quiet, dark area on a dirt road that appeared deserted.

At that spot, they lowered the metal runners from the back

of the flatbed trailer, untied the Jones truck, and pushed it off.

Collins had no idea where they were. They got back in the company truck, Collins again behind the wheel, and drove off, leaving the bullet-riddled yellow truck on the road.

Howard Collins did not get his bearings until they reached the interstate highway. At that point, he glanced at his watch and remembered later that it was about eighteen minutes after eleven.

Hubert Jr. then gave him directions through some back roads to the town of Spring Hill. There, they parked the company truck in front of the home of Mary Ann Moore, Hubert's girlfriend. They removed some of the guns from the company truck and put them in Hubert's personal truck that was parked in the yard at Mary Ann's house.

The machine gun was packed between some clothing in the toolbox in the bed of Hubert's truck. The guns that had been in Larry Gene Jones' truck, the single-shot shotgun and the lever action rifle, were left in the company truck. Mary Ann Moore heard them and came to the door. They went into the house. Hubert Jr. and Mary Ann went into the bedroom. Collins sat down in the living room. He thought he waited there about thirty or forty minutes. He was in an agitated state. He couldn't sit still. He would get up and pace around the room, sit down for a few minutes, then get to his feet again. The wound in his arm throbbed. When he lit a cigarette, his hands were trembling. Beads of cold sweat were glistening on his forehead.

The events of the past hours had left him badly shaken; The visions of the Jones man lying on the ground and the two boys kneeling under the guns of the Wards were burned into his mind. Jones had been lying very still. Was he dead or just passed out? What was going to happen to the boys? He was terrified at the danger he was in, himself. He had been involved in a shoot-out over marijuana. What would happen to him if the law came into this thing? He'd never been in this kind of trouble before in his life. He hadn't asked for this. He wished he could push a magic button and have it all turn into a bad dream.

He was still frightened about his own safety. The events of the past hours demonstrated to him how dangerous the Ward people could be if threatened or crossed. He was a witness. Was he going to be allowed to live?

He could hear Hubert Jr. and Mary Ann talking in the bedroom. After a half hour or so, they came out. Mary Ann prepared a breakfast for them of biscuits and sausage, then she said she had to go to work. She had a job on the early shift at a cafe.

The two men then lay down. Collins fell into a fitful sleep of exhaustion. At 8:30, they got up and started driving to Arab, Alabama. Hubert Jr. drove his personal truck. Howard Collins followed behind in the company truck, which was still pulling the flatbed trailer.

A mile out of Spring Hill, Hubert Jr. pulled to the side of the road beside some dumpsters. Howard stopped behind him. Hubert Jr. came around to the cab window of the truck Howard was driving. He said he wanted them to take off their shoes and throw them into the dumpster. He said they might have left tracks back at the site of the shoot-out, and he didn't want anything that would connect them with what had happened on the Ward farm.

Again, Howard did as he was told. He removed his loafers and tossed them in the dumpster. As he did so, he noticed a survey man some distance away with his instruments aimed in their direction. He wondered if Hubert Jr. was aware of the witness, but thought it best to say nothing. Hubert Jr. got a pair of boots out of his truck and loaned them to Collins.

Then they were on the interstate. Collins remained behind Hubert's truck. After a few miles, they doubled back one time, made a turn around and went back up the interstate a short way, then turned around and went back down it a short way. They made a lot of turns and backtracking. Collins didn't understand the reason for all the extra driving, but followed obediently.

Once, they stopped for fuel. Collins drank a coke and ate some cookies. After some more driving, they pulled off the road in a lonely area. Hubert Jr. got out and threw the black pistol with the white handle as far as he could into a field. Then he asked Collins to hand him the single-shot shotgun. These were the guns that had been in Larry Gene Jones' truck at the shoot-out back at the Ward farm. Hubert Jr. also threw the shotgun into the weeds of the field.

They then drove on to Arab, Alabama, where Bobby Ward was in charge of the job site. They parked the trucks. Hubert Jr. went into the construction office to talk to his son, Bobby. Collins later said they talked for a long time. This was the morning of September 4.

Collins then went with Hubert Jr. to Opelica, where they finished out the week, working on a job. At the end of the week, they returned to Arab where Collins picked up his car. He drove to Birmingham to visit a brother. The gunshot wound in his arm was troubling him. His brother probed for the shotgun pellet and was able to remove it.

Howard Collins couldn't shake the dreadful feeling that, back in the Hartsville area, events were moving to a powerful whirlpool that was going to suck him into its black depths.

Chapter 8

September 17

During the days following the discovery of Larry Jones' bullet-ridden truck, the TBI agent, Frank Evetts, had been busy interrogating tobacco cutters and farmers in Trousdale County. Evidence was piling up. It pointed in one direction: marijuana was being grown on the Jerry Ward farm. The vision Carl Shoopman, the psychic, had about the truck and the Ward farm, while not admissible in court, helped convince Evetts that he needed to have the Jerry Ward farm searched.

On September 17, a search warrant was obtained. The warrant gave the law officers the legal right to search the Ward property for signs of marijuana. At 9:30 that morning, Evetts went to the Ward farm. Sheriff Robinson followed soon after.

They found much of the farm grown up in grass and weeds higher than a man could see over except for an area near the barn that had been cleared with a mowing machine called a bush hog. This was the area behind a walled-in area on one side of the barn. Robinson saw that the wall was about twelve feet high. It had three sides, the barn being the fourth. The boards were butted tightly together. On the back side of the wall, a portion had been knocked or torn down.

Robinson found that Jerry Ward was the only member of the family on the farm that morning. He said his wife Melinda was in Illinois and his mother was visiting relatives in Lafayette.

Evetts and Robinson inspected the space inside the walled area and the barn. The evidence was overwhelming. Robinson arrested Jerry Ward on a charge of cultivating and growing marijuana. He put Jerry Ward in his sheriff's car and took him to the Hartsville jail where he was locked in a cell. At that time it was 11:30 in the morning.

Sheriff Robinson had lunch in the living quarters of the jail. After lunch, he made two calls, then returned to the jail. He walked into the area where the cell blocks were situated. Jerry Ward had been placed in one of the cells with other prisoners.

Robinson moved Ward to the drunk tank, which was empty, so they could have some privacy. The sheriff advised Jerry of his rights. Then he said, "Jerry, I want to talk to you about what happened on your place a couple of weeks ago, on September 3. Do you know Larry Gene Jones from Macon County?"

Ward nodded.

"You know, he and his son and nephew have been missing since September the 3. Now, I've talked to some people who say that Larry Gene sneaked onto your place about a week before that, trying to get to that marijuana. Your wife ran him off. On the afternoon of September 3, Larry Gene Jones and the two boys drove off somewhere in Jones' pickup truck. They never came back. Nobody knows what happened to them. We've found Jones' truck shot up real bad. The crime lab identified traces of marijuana in the bed of the truck."

As the sheriff talked, he was observing Jerry Ward closely. He could see that Ward was growing increasingly depressed and nervous.

Ward was rubbing his damp palms on his trousers. He was staring down at the floor. He mumbled, "Sheriff, if I knew where the bodies were, I would tell you."

It was obvious to Robinson, a trained lawman, that Ward was lying and that he was near the breaking point. Sheriff Robinson later said, "After I had talked to Jerry and interviewed him for several minutes, I saw then, being a police officer for twenty-three years and interviewing hundreds of people, I saw that Jerry was ready to tell me what happened. So, I wanted a witness since this was such a serious offense. So I left there, went back to the Ward farm, and got Agent Evetts. This was approximately 1:40 or 1:45in the afternoon.

"I got Agent Evetts; we came back to the jail. I went in the back and got Jerry, brought him into the living quarters, and when you come into the living quarters, there's a leather chair sitting just inside the door. Agent Evetts sat down in that chair. Jerry sat down on my couch, and I sat down on the end of it beside Jerry, maybe three feet from him.

"Frank Evetts, the TBI agent, then asked Jerry if he'd been advised of his rights, and he told him that he had. And they had a conversation of a little bit, and then we got into the questioning. And just before 2:30,I told Jerry that I thought it would be best if he told us the truth and we get the district attorney. So at that time, Jerry told me to go and call the D.A.

"I went into the office, tried to call the district attorney, General Thompson, who was in court in Gainsboro, and the clerk's line was busy. So I went back and forth two or three times probably, then I got through to the clerk's office, and the district attorney wasn't in the clerk's office, but he told me he'd have him call. And after a While, General Thompson called the jail. I talked with the general. He left immediately, and he and the assistant D.A., General Wooten, arrived at the jail.

"After we had the D.A. and his assistant at the jail, Jerry gave us an oral statement as to what happened out there. And then after he had given us an oral statement, Agent Evetts took a written statement.

"Then he made some kind of statement to us like, 'I'm glad it's over,' 'Glad it's out in the light,' or something similar to this."

The following is the written statement Jerry Ward signed

that day:

"September 17, 1985.I, Jerry Lawrence Ward, do make the following statement, after being advised of my rights.

"I was at home on September the 3, 1985at about 4:00p.m. I was getting off the porch when three men pulled up and said they wanted a drink of water. One then pulled a pistol out and said he wanted to talk to me and my mother. I knocked the pistol out of his hand and started running. I went across the fence toward my trailer. The older man followed and told the two boys to shoot. They were all shooting. I went to my trailer and knocked on the door and told my wife. I then yelled for some help. One of the company trucks was at the tobacco barn. It was my dad and a man who worked for him. My dad came and met me. He had a shotgun. We went down my drive. The truck with the men in it had run over my gate and fence and the board fence around the marijuana. They had loaded the marijuana on the truck and started out and got stuck on the fence below the barn. They started shooting again when they saw us. We, my dad and I both started shooting. All three of them were shot at the truck. I carried them into the hall of the barn and buried them. My dad put the truck on the large company truck and left it until dark. He later carried it out and parked it. I would never have shot them if they had not tried to kill me. I would have called the sheriff if it had not been for the marijuana. The shotgun that I was shooting I had borrowed from Thomas East. I don't know what happened to the guns that they had. I thought they were in the truck when it was parked. The older fellow was acting crazy. I think he was drunk or doped up."

At that point, Sheriff Robinson thought that what he was dealing with was a shoot-out between two groups of armed individuals. It wouldn't be until later that afternoon that he discovered it was more than that-it was one of the most chilling, cold-blooded and brutal assassinations in the state's crime history.

When the sheriff asked for the whereabouts of Jerry's father, Hubert Ward Jr., he learned that he was on a job in Centerville. They had just started a water plant about two weeks before. Robinson immediately got on the telephone and called the sheriff at Centerville and asked him to go out and ask Mr. Hubert Ward Jr. to come to Hartsville and bring the man with him that was over there on September 3. That man was Howard Collins.

Hubert Ward Jr. agreed to be at the district attorney's office that night at 7 o'clock with Howard Collins.

After Jerry Ward had signed the written confession, he told the officers where the bodies of Larry Gene Jones, Mickey Jones, and Kenny Summers could be found. He said that if the officers went into barn and went to the second stall on the left, that three people were buried in a shallow grave, all in the same grave, and that they were just barely under the top of the straw.

Robinson later said, "Before I went, I stopped up at Dr. Carey's office. Dr. Bratton, the medical examiner, was out of town. Dr. Carey was his assistant. I asked him to come over there.

"Then I stopped on the way over at the ambulance service and asked the ambulance people to bring the proper material that they needed to handle the situation and to come on over, and they did. I got over there at approximately 3:30 and Officer Moore and another one or two had just gotten the tin away from the door, or had just gotten it opened when 1 got there, because I had to stop at these two places. And when I went in the front of the barn, went to the second stall on the left, and when I walked in, I could see the shirt of the boy that was on the top."

Chapter 9

The afternoon of September 17

It was mid-afternoon. The newspaper editor, Hal Bevans, hurried out of his office and stopped at Jake Nixon's desk. "I just got a call from a deputy in Trousdale County. There's been a break in the missing person case. They've gotten a confession from Jerry Ward. You'd better get over to the Ward farm right away. They're on their way to search for the bodies."

Bodies.

Jake felt a deep stab of sympathy for the families of the missing boys that he had interviewed. Through his interviews and stories, he had come to know the families well and think of them as friends. They were simple, decent, hard working people. The death of those two teenage boys was going to be something they'd never get over.

They had been clinging to the forlorn hope that Mickey and Kenny might still be alive somewhere. For some time, Jake had realistically given up that hope. He'd become convinced that the trio was dead. Carl Shoopman, the psychic, believed they were dead. The only question was what had happened to the bodies.

Jake remembered what Carl Shoopman had said about the Ward farm. He had told Jake, "There was gunfire there. A lot of gunfire. I pointed to the area of the barn and shed, and I told the officers that there was a clue there that would solve the case. I had some real strong feelings about those out buildings. I told the officers that they'd need to talk to those people that lived there. I thought they knew a whole lot about what happened to those three missing people."

Jake felt a chill. He'd never again doubt the uncanny ability of a gifted psychic like Carl Shoopman.

"Did you get any particulars about what happened?" he asked.

Bevans shook his head. "All I know is that Jerry Ward confessed to some kind of shoot-out on his farm on September the third and said the bodies could be found in the barn."

"I'm on my way," Jake said.

"I'm sending a photographer with you."

"Okay. Tell him to meet me in the parking lot."

When Jake and the photographer arrived at the Ward farm, they found a small crowd milling around. There were a number of police cars and an ambulance parked in the yard near the barn. The TBI agent, Frank Evetts, was on the scene. The assistant medical examiner arrived.

Jake saw that his newspaper hadn't been the only media that had been tipped off. Other reporters and a television van were present. They were prepared for an unpleasant sight. No one was prepared for the gruesome horror the next two hours would bring.

Jake and his photographer hurried into the musty-smelling barn. Sheriff Ashe's deputy, Philip Moore, was in the hallway of the barn. The second stall on the left was boarded up. The latch was tied. A sheet of tin was nailed over the stall door.

Photographers' cameras flashed as Moore worked to pry the tin loose from the door. There was the sound of Moore's hammer and pry bar ripping loose tin and boards. Jake moved closer as the door was opened. He looked in on a stall about eight feet wide by eight feet long. He was aware of a heavy, unpleasant odor in the place.

His gaze was drawn to the shallow grave. It was dark and dingy in the stall, but he could see a mound of dirt, straw and manure, a white substance, and a portion of a decaying body. He shuddered. .

More cameras flashed as the deputy and ambulance people put on rubber gloves and face masks. They shoved aside some of the loose dirt and began pulling out the first body. Jake and the television crew were ordered back out of the way as the first body was brought out.

Then Jake saw something shocking. The hands and feet of the body were bound with wire. From the shoulders up, the body had decayed so that it had very little form. About all that Jake could make out was that it had a head. He'd always thought he had a strong stomach, but he felt a wave of nausea.

Then the second body was dragged out into the hall. Jake stared at it, finding it hard to believe what he saw. The victim's hands were tied behind him, his feet were tied at his ankles, and there was a rotting gag in what had been his mouth.

"This doesn't look like the result of a shoot-out to me," he muttered to his photographer. "It's starting to look like some kind of cold-blooded, ritual execution."

He realized his photographer's face was taking on a pale greenish tinge. Jake felt sorry for him. He was a kid in his early twenties. In his newspaper career, Jake had seen some gruesome killings, but this was beginning to get to him, too.

At that point the bodies had not been identified. The features of the second victim, too, had decomposed beyond recognition. However, there was visible a tattoo on the chest that later identified him as Larry Gene Jones.

The third body was lying on its back. The left leg was straight. The right leg was bent up some and twisted to the right. Again, as with the first two, the hands and feet were tied with wire and a gag was stuffed in the mouth.

After the bodies had been removed, Jake could see how

shallow the grave was-only about a foot deep. He was relieved to get out of the fetid, rotting atmosphere of the barn into some fresh air. His photographer was walking on rubbery legs. Jake thought a few more minutes in the barn and the kid would have passed out. The TV camera crew was busy filming the scene as the bodies, covered now, were taken from the barn to the waiting ambulance.

Jake's photographer gamely took several more pictures, then went around to the side of the barn and threw up. Jake thought that he, too, was very close to losing his lunch. He realized his hands were shaking as he lit a cigarette. He wished he had a drink.

Altogether, it took more than two hours to get the bodies out of the grave and into the ambulance. Jake stayed at the scene for another hour, interviewing the law officials who would talk to him. Then he returned to the newspaper office.

He walked into his editor's office and sank heavily into a chair.

"My God, you look awful," Bevans exclaimed.

"You ought to see the photographer. Have you got something to drink around here?"

"Coffee?" the editor asked, getting up from his desk.

"Do you have anything to put in it?" Bevans opened a desk drawer. "I keep a small bottle of sour mash bourbon for emergencies."

"Well, I think this would qualify. I've just seen a sight that turned my blood cold. Did you say Jerry Ward had confessed to some kind of shoot-out at his place on the third?"

"That's as much as the deputy I talked with could tell me."

Jake shook his head. "What I saw was no shoot-out. It was a cold-blooded execution. Hal, those boys had their hands tied behind them with wire. Their feet were tied with wire. They were gagged. And then, from what I could see, their heads were half blown off. Then they were put in a shallow grave less than a foot deep and covered with lime, straw, and dirt."

"Good Lord," Bevans whispered. His hand shook as he handed Jake the coffee.

"Thanks."

"I'd sure like to know what happened at the Ward place that day of the shooting."

"So would I," Jake agreed. "I was able to get a little more information out of the law people that were at the barn this afternoon. It looks like Jerry Ward's father, Hubert Ward Jr., and a man who works for him named Howard Collins were all involved in the affair. That's in addition to Jerry Ward and his wife, Melinda. Sheriff Robinson located Jerry's father and Howard Collins, and they have agreed to come in to talk to the district attorney this evening. I sure hope in the next few days I can interview them. I also want to see what the coroner finds out when he examines the bodies. Maybe that will tell us something about what really happened. A deputy told me that, according to Jerry Ward's story, there was a big shoot-out between the Wards and Larry Jones. He said the three were killed in the exchange of gunfire, and that he hid the bodies in the barn because of his illegal marijuana crop. That's not what I saw today. Those three people were tied hand and foot, gagged, and then executed. The big question in my mind is why, and who did the cold-blooded killing?"

Chapter 10

Kenny' mother told how she heard about the bodies being found:

"Each of us heard about it in a different way. The way I first heard about it was when one of Kenny's brothers drove up in a car with a friend and came into the house and asked, 'Have they been over here and told you anything?'

"And I said, 'No.' And he said, 'Well, they found Kenny. They found him in the Ward barn.'

"I said, 'Are they alive?'

"He said, 'No.' He said, 'They are buried in that barn.'

"I said, 'Tommy, that is just another one of those rumors that are going around.'

"He said, 'No, it's not. It's on the news.'

"Then I looked out to the car where his friend was sitting and he had his head on his arm on the steering wheel and he was crying.

"Then Sheriff Mercer drove up. He came in the house and he told me that Kenny was dead. He's a big, strong man, but he was crying when he told me about my boy. He said he had a son about Kenny's age and could imagine him in that grave.

"several friends come over during that time. They had seen it on the news. Wayne went to the sheriff's office and when he got back he had a copy of where he had signed for them to do an autopsy on the body.

"Then we had to round up Kenny's brothers and tell them about it. Kenny's sister Patricia more or less went off her rocker, and we were having an awful time trying to calm her down.

"Then after they took the bodies to Nashville, we really didn't know how they were shot or anything. Sheriff Mercer told me that when he did find out, he would come and he would tell me everything. In the meantime we were hearing different stories on the news. We heard on one story that one of them was gagged. They all had their hands and feet tied and one of them was gagged. Actually, all three of them were gagged. We found that out later, and all these stories were going around-like they said Larry's tongue was hanging out where he had tried to work his tongue out of that gag. And they were telling that Kenny was rolled up in barbed wire, and just all kinds of wild rumors like that were going around.

"Then Sheriff Mercer come out again to talk to us and told me, he said, 'Well, your son hadn't suffered. He died fast. He was shot in the head.' But he didn't tell me then that Kenny was shot in the head more than once. He and Mickey were shot in the head with a shotgun and with a pistol. They put the shotgun in his mouth and shot him. The bodies were placed in the custody of the State of Tennessee and taken to Nashville for an autopsy. Larry was identified by his tattoos and the stuff in his wallet. Mickey was identified by his dental records and wallet. They knew the third one had to be Kenny.

"They found them on Tuesday, but it was Friday night before they finally got the bodies back up here. Of course, we couldn't see them. They had them in plastic bags."

September 20

On Friday evening, the Alexander Funeral Home in Lafayette was notified and they went to Nashville and picked up the bodies. The bodies would have been taken directly to the graves because of the odor problem, but the funeral home was able to provide a special mummy-type case called a Ziegler case with a rubber seal. The bodies were placed in these cases, tightly sealed, and then placed in closed caskets.

On Saturday, September 21, the three caskets were at the chapel in the Alexander Funeral Home in Lafayette. All day, a steady crowd of friends and acquaintances came to pay their respects. The chapel was a mass of flowers.

At dusk, ten friends and relatives escorted Mickey's casket from the chapel of the Alexander Funeral Home to a waiting hearse that carried him to the Crow Funeral Home in Glasgow, Kentucky, for funeral services in the city where his mother lived.

On Sunday, September 22; services for Larry and Kenny were held in Lafayette. The service was conducted as if all three victims were present. Reverend Charles Mayes spoke.

So many relatives were present that the family nook could not hold them all. The family was seated in the main chapel. Several poems written by friends and classmates were read. The funeral home was packed. There was standing room only inside with more people gathered outside the entrance and in the parking lot. The line of cars to the cemetery was over a mile long.

At one time, during the funeral, Mickey's grandmother Inez had a fainting spell. Polly Summers appeared to be in a trance. She did not break down or shed a tear. She told her family that she had to stay strong. If she gave in to her emotions, it would spread to the other family members.

Larry Gene Jones and Kenny Summers were buried at the Roark Cemetery in Lafayette.

Jake Nixon attended the services in Lafayette. The next morning, Monday, September 23, Jake drove to Glasgow for Mickey's funeral.

It was a cloudy, overcast day with a steady, drizzling rain. Reverend Darwin Bostwick of the Assembly of God Church gave the eulogy. He opened the service with his memory of a quiet boy with a smile for everyone. He read a poem that one of Mickey's school friends had written. It described Mickey as a quiet, well-liked boy who would not soon be forgotten.

At the graveside services in Memorial Gardens, Jake stood in the crowd under an umbrella. There was a rumble of thunder. The clouds were heavy, the day was dark. Rain drummed on the umbrellas and dripped from the canopy over the grave.

A line William Shakespeare had penned came to Jake's mind: "Woe to the hand that shed this costly blood."

Chapter 11

Jake Nixon became aware of something damp and warm nuzzling the back of his neck. He awoke groggily and sat up. Greeting him with a wagging tail was a large dog of mixed brown and white colors and indeterminate ancestry. Jake' rubbed the animal's shaggy head. "'Morning, Hindenburp. Time for breakfast, huh?"

The dog gave him a tongue-lolling grin of affection.

Jake was not a morning person. He woke up slowly in various stages and degrees. The first stage consisted of groping on the bedside table for his glasses, wristwatch, and crumpled pack of cigarettes. He smoked his first cigarette of the day as he sat on the side of the bed. At that stage, his mind was still cloudy and befuddled. His entire being ached to crawl back under the covers. With a struggle, he mustered his willpower and went on to the next stage, which was stumbling into the bathroom and taking a shower. At that point the day began to come into focus. He had his first strong cup of coffee while shaving. Life took on a clearer image. By the time he was dressed, sitting at the kitchen table having his third cup of coffee and second cigarette, he was fully and completely awake, all the circuits in his brain operational.

Jake lived on the edge of town in a small, frame house which he rented by the month. He had tried living in apartments after his divorce, but it was never satisfactory. He liked the freedom of coming home late and turning up the volume of his record player, a practice that had met with severe disapproval by apartment managers. Also, it was hard to find an apartment that would allow him to keep his roommate, Hindenburg. One look at the big, shaggy dog, and apartment managers grimly shook their heads.

The rented house worked out fine. Jake didn't bother the neighbors and they didn't bother him. He also didn't bother with any housekeeping. Gradually, the clutter and refuse of daily living, the newspapers, filled ashtrays, dirty laundry, frozen dinner trays, and magazines reached proportions that required professional help. At that point, about once a month, Jake called in a housekeeper who brought industrial strength cleaning aids and restored a semblance of order.

Hindenburg had been Jake's companion for the past five years. Jake had watched a television documentary of the Hindenburg zeppelin disaster the night his dog, still a puppy, had knocked over a stack of dishes with a crash. The name seemed appropriate, and became more so as the dog grew into a huge, clumsy, walking disaster.

Jake gave Hindenburg his morning rations of dog food. As he was leaving for work, he walked past a picture that he had hung on a wall near the door. It was a picture of a young, happy family, a proud mother and father with two small children. This had been his family a lifetime ago. It was one of the reasons he had become so emotionally involved with the murder of the two teenage boys, Mickey Jones and Kenny Summers. When he looked at the little boy in the picture on his wall, the picture of his son, he understood all too well the grief of the families of the two murdered boys.

Several weeks had passed since the funeral of Larry Gene Jones, Mickey Jones, and Kenny Summers. A grand jury had convened and had indicted Jerry Lawrence Ward, Melinda Ward, and Hubert Ward Jr. on first degree murder charges.

Jake had made a number of trips to Hartsville, Nashville and Pell City, Alabama. He had talked to a lot of people, had dug into a lot of court records. The more answers he found, the more questions he uncovered. He had opened a Pandora's box.

Now, Jake Nixon drove into the newspaper parking lot. In the building, he tapped at the city editor's office door,   then entered .

Hal Bevans glanced up from his desk. '"Morning, Jake." He settled back in his swivel chair. He knew the reporter was still spending some time on the murder case. Jake had become obsessed with the case. Bevans didn't mind. Nixon was giving him good coverage, and the case was still front page material. "Got anything new on the Ward murder case?"

Jake took a seat. "I'm finding out this thing has more twists and turns than we ever suspected. None of the Wards will talk to me, but I was able to get Howard Collins to open up to me."

Bevans nodded. "Collins is the guy who works for the Ward Construction Company, right?"

"Yeah. His immediate boss in Jerry Ward's father, Hubert Jr. That's a little confusing. Hubert Jr. is actually the senior Ward, but since he was named after his father, he's Hubert Ward Jr. To add to the confusion, one of his sons is Hubert III. At any rate, Collins was at the scene that day on the Ward farm. He'd come down with Jerry's father to get some construction material and got involved in the shootout."

Jake related the events of the afternoon as Collins had described them. Then he added; "Collins swears that when he drove out of the yard with the Jones truck on the flatbed trailer, the boys were still alive. They were on their knees, tied hand and foot with gags in their mouths. If he's telling the truth, they were executed sometime later that night."

"And the Wards have been charged with the murders." Jake nodded. "The grand jury has also indicted Howard Collins as an accessory. The word around the courthouse is that he's going for a plea bargain. His lawyer is trying to make a deal for Collins to turn state's evidence. He could be an important witness for the state. He says he saw Hubert Ward Jr. shoot Larry Gene Jones. He doesn't know who shot the boys, however."

"It must have been Jerry."

Jake shrugged. "Hal, there are a lot of things about this case that are puzzling and downright baffling."

The editor looked at him curiously. "Such as?"

"When Collins drove away from the Ward farm that night with Hubert Ward JR., he says there were three members of the Ward family there with the boys, Jerry, Melinda" and Hubert III. There were apparently a lot of guns around there, pistols, shotguns, even a semiautomatic rifle."

"Do you think they might have all been involved in the execution of the boys?"

"I really don't know enough about the case yet to venture a guess. I'm hoping that what really happened that night will come out in the trial. There are a heck of a lot of unanswered questions.

"From what I've been able to find out at this point, the D.A. plans to try Melinda separately. At first he thought he would try Hubert Jr., Melinda, and Jerry Ward all at the same time. But apparently there are some legal problems involved in that. He intends to try the best case he has first, which is against Jerry Ward and his father, Hubert.

"I've been told that Melinda is the coldest one in the bunch. If anyone of them had the nerve to execute those boys, she probably would be the one. But I have a hunch the D.A. feels it could be tough to get a jury conviction against a woman on purely circumstantial evidence. It's going to be tough enough to get a jury in Trousdale County to convict one of their own."

"How about Hubert Ward III?"

"He claims he was drunk when he got there that night, that he passed out or went to sleep and doesn't know what happened. The grand jury didn't indict him. He waived immunity, so I assume he could still be charged as an accessory."

Jake went on. "Right now, the Wards are all out on bond. Jerry's and Hubert's bond was set at $100,000.Melinda's was $30,000.I found out that Jerry's sister, Byrdie, and her husband, signed the Wards' bond. Nobody has offered to sign for Howard Collins' bond, so he'll probably stay in jail until the trial. I suspect he'd just as soon stay there where it's safe. If he's going to be the state's main witness, he might think it wouldn't be too healthy for him to be on the outside."

"Hmm. Any chance Jerry Ward WIII go for a plea bargain?"
"Doesn't look like it. He's got a damn good defense attorney, Eddie Taylor. The trial will take place in Hartsville. It will be next to impossible to get an impartial jury. The Wards have lived in Trousdale County for several generations. Everyone knows them. Larry and the two boys were from Macon County. They're considered out- siders. The sympathy of people in Trousdale County will be on the side of the Wards. I'm sure Eddie Taylor has taken that into consideration. There's a bitter rivalry between Trousdale and Macon. Those people down there think if you're from Macon County, you don't have any business being in Trousdale County. The feeling I get when I talk to people in Trousdale County is that if Jones and the boys would have stayed home, none of this would have happened. Some people have even recommended to the D.A. that the charges against the Wards be dismissed, since they'd done no more than defend their own homes."

"Cold-bloodedly executing two teenage boys who are tied and gagged goes a long way beyond just defending your home."

"Sure, it does. But y'know this territorial instinct can be

strong. People don't always use reason when they're defending one of their own against outsiders."

Jake was thoughtful for a moment, then he continued, "But aside from all that, there are things about this case that really have me puzzled. Think about it for a minute, Hal. Here's a guy, Jerry Ward, a local boy, living on a dirt farm in a little, isolated rural area. He raises a marijuana crop. Not just any crop, but the very best, high-grade stuff you can find. A crop that has to be worth maybe a million dollars on the street. What is he going to do with it after he gets it harvested? He can't sell it locally. He has to get it to someplace like Nashville or Birmingham. Then what does he do with it? He's not going to stand on a street corner and sell it out of his truck like a crop of watermelons. He has to have some kind of underworld, drug dealer contacts to take the stuff off his hands. Who are they? Nobody seems interested in pursuing that. At one time, bootleg liquor was big business in these rural parts. These days, it's drugs. Where you've got drugs, you've got powerful crime bosses. You've also probably got law officials being paid off. Now, the thing that keeps sticking in my mind is the way Collins described that evening after he'd tied up Jones and the boys. The Wards kept talking among themselves and making phone calls. At one point, one of the boys, Mickey I think, asked what was going to happen to them. The Wards said something like, 'We've got to wait for the big man.' That sounds like they were waiting for somebody higher up to tell them what to do with their captives, doesn't it?"

"Sounds that way," Bevans agreed, nodding.

"The D.A. thinks they were talking about Hubert III. That's possible. He's big physically. But were they talking about someone big physically or big in a different sense? From what Collins told me, it doesn't sound like Hubert III carried much weight in telling anybody what to do. First, he was drunk. Second, his father ordered him out of the way, back to the house, saying, 'We've got work to do,' and he meekly obeyed. No, I think if they were waiting for instructions from somebody higher up, it wasn't Hubert III."

"Got any ideas along that line?"

"Possibly. A mystery figure in all this is Jerry's brother, Bobby Ward. It looks like he holds the purse strings in the family. He owns the trailer house Jerry is living in. He's half owner of the construction company that his father and Howard Collins work for."

The editor looked startled. "You think he was involved in the marijuana crop? That he's the 'big man' in charge?" "This is all theory, you understand. It's just my idea of a possible scenario. The records of the telephone company only show calls made from the Ward farm to Nashville that night. Hubert III lives in Nashville. His father, not wanting any calls made that could be traced, ordered Hubert III to contact the 'big man' about the situation on the Ward farm. Hubert III then went to a phone booth. Who did he call? Let's theorize that he called Bobby Ward in Alabama. I took the time last weekend to drive to Pells City, Alabama, where Bobby was the night of the murders. I found that Bobby would have had time to drive from Pells City to the Ward farm that night. Or, he could have driven the short distance, about twenty-five miles, to Birmingham. There is an evening flight that would have put him in Nashville in an hour. There, he could have rented a car, or maybe Hubert III had one he could use. The same flight returns to Birmingham the next morning. He would have gotten to the Ward farm after Collins and Hubert Jr. left that night and had plenty of time to be back in his office the next morning before his father and Collins got there that day." Jake continued, "That's one possibility. The other, of course, is that the 'big man' is a higher up drug dealer or some political figure on the take."

"Those are all interesting theories," his editor said, "but that's all they are. Theories. You don't have any proof. You can't print any of what you've told me."

"Sure, I know that. Maybe we'll get some answers when the trial begins. The way it stands now, Jerry Ward and his father, Hubert Jr., are scheduled to appear in Trousdale County Criminal Court next April 23 to stand trial for the first-degree murder of Larry Gene Jones, Larry 'Mickey' Jones, and Kenneth Summers. Jerry's wife Melinda will be tried separately on charges of aiding and abetting first degree murder."

After the trial took place, however, there was destined to be an unexpected turn of events that would take Jake completely by surprise.

Chapter 12

April 23, 1986

As the trial began, state newspapers carried front pagestories. From the *Lebanon Democrat,* dateline Wednesday, April 23,1986:

TRIPLE MURDER TRIAL STARTS
1,000Potential Jurors Reviewed,
Attorneys Expect Lengthy Selection

HARTSVILLE-Trial motions are set to begin here Thursday for a man and his son both charged with first degree murder in an execution-style slaying of a Lafayette man, his teenage son and nephew last September. Hubert Ward, 60, and Lawrence Jerry Ward, 30, are scheduled to appear in Trousdale County Criminal Court Thursday morning to begin a lengthy jury selection and trial.

The younger Ward's wife, Melinda Ward, will be tried separately on charges of aiding and abetting first degree murder. A fourth person, Howard Collins of Florida, was charged with aiding and abetting in the September 3 slaying. Collins appeared in Smith County's Criminal Court last Thursday and plea bargained an accessory after the fact charge. He was sentenced to three two-year terms and is eligible for parole in 14 months.

The bodies of the two boys, Jones and Summers, were found bound, gagged, and badly decomposed in a shallow grave in a barn stable on the Ward farm in the Providence community of Trousdale County just a few miles over the Wilson County line, September 17.

April 29, 1986

JUDGE RULES TO SEPARATE TRIALS
FOR DEFENDANTS IN TRIPLE MURDER CASE

HARTSVILLE-An unexpected development in the first degree murder trial of Hubert and Jerry Ward occurred today when Criminal Court Judge Robert Bradshaw ruled that the trial of Hubert Ward would be held separately from the trial of his son, Jerry Lawrence Ward.

Jury selection is scheduled to begin tomorrow in the first degree murder charge against Jerry Lawrence Ward. Officials believe the jury selection process will go quicker now that the trial for Hubert Ward has been set for a later date.

The next day when the court was called to order, the process of jury selection began. Jake Nixon was in the crowded courtroom with his pad and pencil. He wrote a brief description of the people who would play the major roles in the courtroom drama.

"Judge Bradshaw is a man in his mid-sixties, balding, with a fringe of salt-and-pepper hair. He wears horn rimmed glasses. He is medium height, about 5'6".

"The two prosecutors are District Attorney Tom P. Thompson and Assistant District Attorney John Wooten.

"Thompson is tall, 6'3" or more, clean-shaven, well dressed, attractive and mild-mannered. He has a full head of thick brown hair and weighs about 220 pounds. His age-early 40s.

"John Wooten, in his early thirties, has a medium build, is about 5'10", and weighs in the neighborhood of 175 pounds. He has black hair.

"For the defense, Eddie Taylor. Has a reputation as one of

the best defense lawyers in the area. He's a man about thirty years of age, has black hair, a beard and mustache. He weighs about 200 pounds. He is well-groomed and easy-talking."

Then Jake turned his attention to the members of the Ward family in the courtroom. The defendant, Jerry Ward, was a husky man with a dark mustache. He fit the image of the powerfully built man who had once been a high school football star.

Jerry's father, Hubert Ward Jr.,was a six-footer, built lean and hard, weighing about 180 pounds. He had a heavy, drooping mustache and full head of hair. His hair and mustache were so black for a man his age, Jake speculated that he might use some hair dye. Once, he glanced in Jake's direction. Their gazes met for a moment. The eyes Jake saw were cold, unfeeling, callous. Jake thought, "There's a man I wouldn't want mad at me."

Finally, there was Jerry Ward's young wife, Melinda. She was small, about 5'2", and weighed a trim 100pounds. Her dark hair was worn in a short style. Jake thought he would describe her as sexy. She wore a figure-hugging dress with spaghetti straps that bared her shoulders.

Was she a femme fatale? Jake had been told by members of the Jones family not to be miss lead by her young age and petite figure, that she was actually hard as nails. Was that true? If Howard Collins had told him the truth, when he and Hubert Jr. had driven away from the Ward farm that fateful night, the two boys, Mickey and Kenny, were still alive. Jerry's brother, Hubert III, was in the house, drunk, possibly passed out. That left Jerry and Melinda standing guard with their arsenal of guns.

Was one of these people capable of the cold-blooded murder of two teenage boys who were on their knees, tied hand and foot? Were all of them capable of such an inhuman act? Or was there another individual involved who wasn't even in the courtroom?

Was Howard Collins telling the truth?

There were a lot of tantalizing questions. Would the trial provide the answers?

Chapter 13

Because Hubert Ward would now be tried separately, the jury selection went faster than expected. Within four days, a jury of six men and six women had been selected.

The jurors were: Sherrie Dickens, Mary Hawkins, Clara Cook, Teresa Duncan, Rosa Brooks, Terry Dix Dunn, Will Roddy, Kelly Cox, John Valentine, Daniel Rader, Sammy Dixon, and Harold Atterbury. The jury foreman was Will Roddy.

During the jury selection process, some of the potential jurors had been excused because of business or family hardships. Most had been excluded because of preformed opinions or because they were acquainted with the Ward family.

One of those excused was Lyn Cassity, who came into the courtroom with a chip on her shoulder and a very definite opinion about the guilt or innocence of Jerry Ward.

The clash she had with the district attorney was enlightening.

When the court asked her if she had formed or expressed an opinion as to the guilt or innocence of the defendant, she replied, "Well, I formed an opinion based on my own knowledge, not what I read or what I saw...I don't believe that anything could be brought into this courtroom that would convince me that Jerry Ward could even be capable of committing first degree murder. That is my opinion. Nothing I read or nothing I heard. That is my opinion. I don't think anybody could bring anything into this courtroom that would prove to me that he is even capable of first degree murder."

The Court asked, *II* And you know the defendant, Mr. Ward, and his family quite well?"

Ms. Cassity: "I've known Jerry ever since he was born.

I've known his whole family all of my life."

The Court: "And I'm sure you had rather not sit on this jury?"

Ms. Cassity: "I don't think the prosecutor would want me to sit on this jury."

General Thompson: "I would sure like to talk to her, judge."

The Court: "Ma'm, I am obligated to let the attorneys for both sides question you ...."

General Thompson: "I haven't got any questions. I just want to tell you that yesterday you said downstairs that I knew that the marijuana was over there and because of that, you would turn him loose, and you read it in the paper. I've heard enough of that."

Ms. Cassity: "I believe it was written in the paper, and on Channel 2 news the statement that marijuana had been raised for ten years on that farm. Someone correct me if I'm wrong."

General Thompson: "Well, you are the one that said you didn't believe the papers, and that if I said anything like that, it was a bald-faced lie."

Ms. Cassity: "Was it not in the paper and on television?"

The Court: "General, I don't think I need to let this-"

General Thompson: "Well, I'm just tired of her running her mouth downstairs about me, Your Honor."

Ms. Cassity: "You asked me if I read the papers."

Mr. Taylor: "Well, each of you have a right to defend yourself, but not here in open court."

Ms. Cassity: "And we have a right to our own opinion about that."

The Court: "Yes, ma'm. Under the circumstances, Ms. Cassity, I think I need to excuse you from this jury. Thank you, ma'm, for coming ...."

The clash of personalities was amusing, but it also reinforced rumors that marijuana was being grown in Trousdale County right under the authorities' noses for years. Apparently it was common street knowledge that marijuana was being raised on the Ward farm. Everyone seemed to know about it except the authorities. At least, that was the street talk.

Was there anything to the story that marijuana had been grown on the Ward farm for ten years? If there was some truth to it and this wasn't the first crop of marijuana raised on the Jerry Ward farm, it again raised the question: what kind of higher-up drug-dealer connections did Jerry Ward have to market the stuff?

There appeared to be a lot of people in Trousdale County who were of the opinion that if authorities had put a stop to the marijuana trade from the Ward farm, that the murders would not have occurred. They seemed to blame the marijuana for the deaths of Jones and the two boys more than they blamed the Ward family. *May 5, 1986*

The trial began with opening statements from the prosecuting and defense attorneys.

The Court: "Gentlemen, the indictment has been read, the jury has been sworn, and we are now ready to begin the trial. Do you gentlemen care to make opening statements?"

General Thompson: "Briefly, Your Honor."

The Court: "All right. General, you may proceed." General Thompson: "Thank you, Your Honor. May it please the Court, and Ladies and Gentlemen of the jury.

"As we told you all through the voir dire (jury selection), what the attorneys say in any trial is not to be taken as evidence. But before any trial begins, both sides are given an opportunity for an opening statement, which is really nothing more than a preview of what we are going to try to show you. This is going to be a difficult, complicated case. However, there will be a lot of witnesses and there will be a lot of evidence that is introduced, and at times there may be objections and us trying to get one thing or another straightened out, and what I want to do right now is tell you what we expect to put on so you'll have some idea as to the relevancy as we proceed along.

"Now as you understood by the indictment, the charge is first degree murder. There were three victims in this case. One, you'll learn through the evidence, was a man named Larry Jones, a thirty-eight year old man from Macon County, and Kentucky also. A man who had a terrible record. A man who didn't do well, and a man who had served time in the penitentiary on several different occasions. You'll find that on this particular day, and prior to September 3, 1985, he had become familiar with the Ward property over here in Trousdale County on 141,south of town here. That the way he was familiar with this property was through other people from Macon County, who happened to be working in the area cutting tobacco for Bobby Cornwell over across the river on Doctor Bratton's farm. And our evidence will show that while they were working over here, they saw a marijuana patch being grown on the Ward farm where all of this occurred.

"The evidence will show that not only did they tell other people about it, but they went and stole some of the marijuana themselves. This was not just rough-grown marijuana. This was the finest marijuana there is, sinsemillia, And it was in an area all around the barn, and it was hidden by a twelve-foot wall and with weeds, known as Sweet Annie, on the other side, that were about ten feet high, so it was hidden. But the cutters had hauled tobacco over in the area and they'd smelled the marijuana and had seen it. So these tobacco cutters knew it was over there and started getting it. And then Larry Jones, being the person he was, decided that he would go down and try to get some of this marijuana, too. And he brought people to go with him. It wasn't bad enough that he brought people who were maybe his own kind. One day on September 3, drunk and pilled up, he picked up his young son, Mick Jones, who was seventeen years old. Then he got his nephew, Kenneth Summers, who was also seventeen years old, and they headed out to Hartsville.

"The proof will show that all of them were drinking somewhat. Larry Jones more so than the others; the boys were six or seven in the intoximeter. You all have heard that D.W.I.'s being .10 are presumed intoxicated. These boys were 6 or 7. And this was determined by the autopsies later on. That they came down, went to the Ward property. They went in, and Jerry Ward was over at his house, and there's a picture of his house and a sketch of the whole area. They went to his house right there, just drove in. Larry Jones got out of his truck and ran Jerry Ward off from home.

"The proof will show that Jerry Ward had been expecting Larry Jones back because Jones had been there the week before and his wife had shot at him, and he'd left. Jerry Ward had been waiting out in the chicken yard where they have a bunch of coops, and all of you have seen the coops over there. So, seven nights, six nights, or five nights, he spent guarding, waiting for Jones to come back. Instead of destroying his marijuana when Jones found out about it, Jerry was there protecting it.

"And that Larry Jones did run Jerry Ward off his property. Jerry Ward left and went and got his father, and there was a man who happened to be up here that day with his father named Howard Collins.

"Now, Howard Collins, you'll learn; is a man who was from Florida. He worked for Reinhart and Ward Construction

Company, which is a family-owned construction company, and was a general laborer under the direct supervision of Jerry Ward's father, Hubert Ward Jr.

"That Hubert and Collins had been up here that day and that they came south from Lebanon sometime during the afternoon and didn't go over to the home place side. They turned right and went up to a barn. There's a barn and shed on that side of 141, on the left side as you go toward Lebanon. It would be on the right coming towards Hartsville. Directly across from the chicken coops. And that's where the corporation keeps a lot of pipe and fittings and supplies that they use on these various jobs. And that while they were out there they were attending their own business, not doing anything but loading pipe and supplies, and they heard, after they'd been there a while, a motor revving up. Both of them raised up and listened, and then they didn't hear anything else. They didn't hear any shots or anything. Just a motor. They went on back to loading the pipe and supplies and the next thing we'll show is that they heard hollering and screaming, and they looked and it was Jerry Lawrence and Melinda. They had run down from their trailer, which is located about a hundred yards or more up towards Hartsville on 141. That was when Hubert and Collins saw them. They was standing out here in the road. They both went to see what was wrong. Jerry said he'd been shot and people had run him off from home and he wanted some help. Hubert said to Collins to unhook the trailer, and that's what Collins did.

"A citizen of Hartsville, a man by the name of Kenny Scruggs, who was working in Nashville and got off somewhere around 3:30 every afternoon, was coming home from work that afternoon and somewhere around 4:30 passed the location. He saw Jerry and Melinda Ward. They stopped him, sought his help, and sent him to Thomas East's, another person here from Hartsville. To not only get Thomas East but get some guns and help them in their predicament.

"Melinda got in the vehicle with Kenneth Scruggs. They came to Hartsville. Thomas East was not able to return back with them, however, they did get a gun from him, a shotgun. A model 97 old Winchester pump. Went back to the location and there Kenneth Scruggs found Jerry and Howard Collins down at the house. Hubert, in the meantime, had gone to get more guns. So he wasn't there when Scruggs came.

"In a few minutes, they all arrived and determined somebody was in the house and Jerry got his spitfire gun. It looks somewhat like a machine gun, shoots a clip of thirty .45 caliber rounds, and it's semiautomatic. He had that; everybody else had shotguns. There were two pistols at that time; Howard Collins had a pistol and Jerry Ward had a pistol. And the pistol that Jerry had was in fact a pistol that Larry Jones had originally had and Jerry took it away from him.

"After they were there a few minutes, they heard a noise down by the barn. So they came, went through a gate right here out into this chicken yard, and they saw the truck down in this enclosure, which is all the way around the back and side of the barn right there. They saw the truck, and at that point a gun battle took place, both sides shooting at each other. The Wards were trying to retake their property. The truck backed out, got hung on this fence right here, which is the same as this right here. There was a cornfield and you'll see from the pictures that this was just a mess. It was all grown up. Weeds were fence-high all through here. Sweet Annie. It was just a mess all through here, and a cornfield right here.

"The truck backed out. They were up here in the chicken yard. There were shots fired back and forth, and in fact Jones and the boys were captured. And the Wards had them get outside the truck, throw their guns down or pitch their guns down before they got out, and had them put their hands over their heads, come up across this fence into the chicken yard. All of the men were up here, all the victims were down here. Larry Jones being drunk and all, you'll hear, was running his mouth. The boys were being relatively quiet. Except for the fact that they told their age and that they'd be missed at school.

"Kenny Scruggs, who was what I'd call a Good Samaritan, did what anybody would have done up to that point, helped a neighbor. He said after they were captured and he saw what was going on, he said, 'Do you all want me to call the law?'

They said, 'No.' 'Are you sure?' 'No, we can't because of the pot.' Kenny Scruggs will tell you that he said, 'Here, take this shotgun. I'm gone.'

"That is where the horror of this case begins. They stood out there. They kept them under control for some two and a half hours, till dark During this period of time, Larry Jones was running his mouth. You'll also find out that he tried to run and he was shot by Hubert Ward, not by Jerry. He went down, begged for help, asked for his boy to help him, and they wouldn't let the boy help him. Sometime before dark, and after Larry-ran, Hubert sent Jerry to get rope. Jerry did, came back, the rope was bad, rotten, so he went back and got wire. He gave that wire to Howard Collins, said, 'Tie them up.' Howard Collins went down, tied the boys' hands behind their back and their feet together.

"You'll find out through the testimony that Larry Jones never got back up from that point. He stayed down and he was shot in the side. But the boys were there, and they were, in my opinion, they were victims. They were right there; they didn't know what was going to happen. Nobody probably knew what was going to happen at that point. But in any event, the testimony will show that after some time and just before dark, after they were tied up, Hubert Ward left. He stayed gone about fifteen, thirty, forty minutes, and returned. When he returned, Jerry Ward, Melinda Ward, and Howard Collins were still down in the chicken yard. It was dark They were still watching the three people. Larry Jones still on the ground. The young boys were still living at that point.

"Hubert and Jerry got off to the side as they did on several occasions and they sent Howard Collins back up to the truck, which at this time was parked close to this gate that goes into the chicken area. When Hubert returned, the proof will show that he brought the truck down to right in this area.

"Now, this was after dark Hubert Ward stayed down with Jerry for a little while. As Howard Collins came out right here, he ran into another person by the name of Ward. And the proof will show by telephone records, that after the trouble began right here and after they were captured at some time, Hubert Ward III, who we know as Little Hubert, was called in Nashville. And he had been off, the only day he'd been off in a while, and had been at the VFW. and had some drinks, and he was at home when he was called. He was told that there was trouble up there, that they needed him at home. So Hubert, after about ten minutes or so, drove up to Hartsville. You'll also hear that his wife called to check to be sure that was where the call came from, and in fact it was. And then when Collins came up from the gate, he walks into Little Hubert. Little Hubert says, 'Hello. They call me Little Hubert. I'm drunk' Collins said he spoke to him just a minute, and then Hubert walked back towards the house. Hubert Jr., his father, came from the barn, and from that point on, Collins and Hubert Jr. went back down with the company truck that they were driving that Collins had unhooked earlier, got the disabled Jones truck, down where it was disabled, and that he briefly turned the lights on and he did see the two boys on their knees, and Jones was still down. Also, when he saw the two boys on their knees, he saw Jerry Ward ten feet from them, and Melinda Ward at a short distance behind him. I don't think he says exactly it was Melinda.

"In any event, the proof will show that they pulled this truck out, loaded it on the trailer that they'd brought up earlier in the day to put the supplies on. And they made a considerable amount of noise, and Jerry Ward came up and jumped all over his daddy for making all the noise and told them to hold it down. That they talked for a while, and then he and Hubert left pulling the trailer, that by this time had the truck loaded on it. And that they headed towards Hartsville on 141 and took a sharp right at the first right which would have been back towards Providence, the Providence Church area, where 414 hits that Providence Road, and that they went back over in Wilson County on a gravel road and at that point the truck was abandoned.

"And at this time, you'll learn it was somewhere after eleven o'clock. That was the last time anybody that I know of saw the two young boys alive.

"Now when the Jones family, the grandmother and Mrs. Summers, realized that their boys didn't come back, of course they reported the children and Larry Jones missing.

"On September 7, the truck was found over in Wilson County, out from Taylorsville, in an abandoned area. It had some marijuana in it and was shot up. It was hauled into Lebanon. Various people from the TBI lab were sent up.

"During this period of time, after they were reported missing, you'll learn that Sheriff Mercer in Macon County and Sheriff Robinson in Trousdale County and Frank Evetts, the TBI agent assigned to this county, interviewed everybody that was foreign in the area, you might say. They had learned about these boys over there cutting tobacco, and there was one girl over there, helping them. And through these interviews, they learned about Jones' previous trip, and the tobacco cutters stealing the marijuana. And they also learned through these interviews that Jerry Ward had seen the truck that Larry Jones was in. That he, in fact, got Thomas East and, both of them armed, went down to where the boys and the girl were cutting tobacco. Jerry Ward got Jones' name and information from these kids about who he was and from that point until the next week, he did wait for Jones to come back.

"After talking to the tobacco cutters and after finding the truck that was shot up, there was sufficient evidence for Agent Evetts to obtain a search warrant. And on September 17, this search warrant was executed with officers in Macon and Trousdale and Wilson County all participating in the search of Jerry Ward's farm.

"The first thing that they did find, you'll find out, was that this area had been bush hogged in the meantime, but the officers found sufficient evidence-some marijuana that remained there. Sheriff Robinson came over about five minutes to twelve and placed Jerry Ward under arrest. Melinda Ward, you'll find out, was in Illinois. Jerry was there by himself working, or doing something. Anyway, he was taken into the jail and the sheriff advised him of his rights and talked to him and realized that he was ready to talk. The sheriff went back and got Agent Evetts, and you'll learn that Jerry Ward gave a statement in the jail that day, about 2:30in the afternoon to the effect that there had been a shoot-out, that these people were killed in the shoot-out, and that he drug them into the barn and buried them. He later told them exactly where they were buried and what type of grave they were in. And as a result of that statement, the sheriff and the TBI agent came back to the barn. The bodies were uncovered.

"This is also where the second horror of this thing comes to. It was dark and dingy in the barn and hard to tell. The bodies were covered with manure and dirt and a white substance. And it was not a pleasant place for anybody to be that day, but still everybody thought maybe it was a shoot-out, until lo and behold, when the second person come out, and you could see enough of him, you could see that he had a gag all the way in his mouth and tied around his head. And that his arms were wired behind him, and that his legs were wired together. They went and looked back at the first one, and sure enough, his arms and legs were wired together. Lo and behold, the third one came out, and the third one that came out was Larry Jones' son, Mick. He was also gagged. His hands were wired together and his feet were wired together.

"Terrible, terrible sight.

"At this point, you'll learn that the officers knew that more people were involved and, from Jerry Ward's statement, they learned that Hubert Ward had been up there and also an employee of Hubert Ward had been up there that day. So the sheriff found where they were working, which was down in Hickman County, and sent word to the sheriff to have Hubert call him. In any event, Hubert Ward agreed to surrender himself through his attorney at that time, Eddie Taylor, and I think attorney Jacky Bellar. Hubert was turned in that night. Whenever he drove up, Mr. Collins was also taken into custody at that point. And the proof will show that Mr. Collins was taken from Eddie Taylor's office, around up Court Street right to the district attorney's office. Within two hours, he gave a statement. On the following Sunday, he gave a more complete statement. He went through the location to the farm with the officers and showed them where everything occurred and what had happened as best he could. He also went with the officers to show them where Hubert had thrown the guns out on the way to Alabama where they had gone the day after the shooting. They disposed of their shoes at a dumpster and happened to see a survey crew, and the survey crew will be here to say that they were surveying in that area that day.

"Also the proof will show that other marijuana was found. That Collins stayed with the officers about three or four days and that as a result, the entire evidence was sent to the grand jury. An indictment was obtained on the four people involved. Hubert III, you'll learn, because he'll testify in this case, that he too went to the grand jury, and in Tennessee, when a person who is a possible defendant goes to a grand jury, they're immune from prosecution, however, he waived his immunity and let whatever he said in the grand jury to be used against him if the grand jury felt that it should, to indict him. They elected not to indict him that day.

"So, four people were indicted: Jerry Ward, Melinda Ward, Hubert Ward, and Howard Collins.

"We are here today to try Jerry Ward, the person who was in possession of the property, the person who was raising the marijuana, and I submit to you, the person, who because of, we have three dead individuals in this county, two of which were nothing more than executed.

"Thank you."

The Court: "Thank you, General. Mr. Taylor?"

Mr. Taylor: "May it please the Court. Ladies and gentlemen of the jury:

"Jerry Ward didn't kill anybody. I'm not going to stand

here and go through all the proof that you're going to have
for the next three, four, five days. General Thompson told you
some of it, and you heard all the things he told you just now.
But not one time did he tell you that Jerry Ward shot and killed
Kenneth Summers. Shot and killed Mickey Jones. Shot and
killed Larry Eugene Jones. In fact, he told you that Jerry Ward
didn't shoot and kill Larry Gene Jones.

"Now the proof will show this: the proof will show that
Lawrence Ward wasn't at his house. He was at his mother's
house, which is this house right here. That Lawrence Ward
certainly wasn't waiting for Larry Jones then, because when
he walked out on the front porch of his mother's house, Larry
Jones stuck a gun in his chest and told him he wanted to talk
to him and his mamma. Jerry Ward got away, ran through a
fence back here, down a ravine, through a bunch of briars and
up to his trailer. And then he saw his father and Collins over at
the barn-that's on down highway 141, back over here. He was
bloody. The proof will show that. And he thought he'd been
shot at the time. And Kenny Scruggs did come by and they
did go to Thomas East and try to get him to come over and he
couldn't come at that time, and I think that will come out in
the proof as to why. They came back with a shotgun and there
was a shoot-out.

"Now, nowhere in this proof, through all these days, will you
ever hear that Jerry Lawrence Ward shot anybody. Lawrence
Ward again was at his mother's house. He was at home and
he lived in a trailer which is right here and his mother lives
right here. Wasn't any further for him to go. "Now, you're
going to hear a lot of testimony and as I say, this thing will
last three or four days. But when it's over, you'll still want to
know who did the shooting. Because, as I told you, there will
be no proof that Jerry Ward did. "Now, last week during the

voir dire, when we were questioning you all, you all told me and you told Jerry and you told the district attorney that you presumed Jerry Lawrence Ward innocent. You also told Jerry Ward and you told me and you told the district attorney that you would make them prove to your satisfaction beyond any reasonable doubt that Jerry Ward killed those three people. You told us that. We believed you then and we believe you now. And you've heard a thirty minute opening statement from the district attorney and he's told you right here and now that he still can't say that Jerry Lawrence Ward did anything. The facts are that you're going to see that there were several other persons over there. He's talked to you about some of them. But when it all comes down, the proof will not be there and again we believed you when you said you wouldn't send us to the penitentiary for life unless they proved our guilt and they can't do it because we ain't guilty.

"Thank you."

The Court: "Thank you, Mr. Taylor.

"Ladies and Gentlemen of the Jury, you've heard the opening statements made by the attorneys for either side. We're ready now to begin with the proof, with the exception that it's almost time for lunch and we wouldn't have time to get into the proof. I suggest we recess court until one o'clock. You ladies and gentlemen go have your lunch and then at one a' clock, we'll begin with the proof in the case."

The six men and six women who filed out of the jury box would, in a few days, add a totally unexpected and bizarre twist ending to this strange case. They would stun everyone involved. They would set a new legal precedent.

Chapter 14

When the court reconvened, the State called its first witness, Sheriff Charles Robinson.

Under questioning by the prosecuting and defense attorneys, Robinson detailed his part in the case, beginning with the disappearance of the trio from Macon County. He related how he had questioned tobacco cutters in the area. They had told him of the marijuana crop at the Ward farm. He told about arresting Jerry Ward on a marijuana charge and then about Ward's confession. Ward's signed statement was read to the court.

Robinson then described finding the bodies and the subsequent arrest of Hubert Ward Jr. and Howard Collins. He also talked about interrogating a man named Lloyd Wrinkle and picking up a gun from Wrinkle that Hubert Ward Jr. had borrowed from him on the day of the shooting, September 3. He then described a visit he made to the home of Thomas East.

Robinson said, "In my investigation, I had learned that Melinda Ward and Kenny Scruggs had gone to Thomas East and borrowed a shotgun from Thomas and then had gone back to the Ward property. The first time I talked to Thomas, I couldn't take a statement from him."

"Why?"

"Thomas was very much intoxicated, and we couldn't take a statement from him."

"At a later date was a statement taken from Thomas?"

"At a later date a statement was taken."

There were no startling revelations in Sheriff Robinson's testimony. For the most part, it was the statement of a professional law officer giving a careful description of the Ward property and a detailed account of the investigation and arrests. It did implicate Kenneth Scruggs and Thomas East as peripheral figures in the events of September 3, and arouse some questions as to just how involved they had been.

Then the State called its principal witness, Howard Collins. The courtroom became tense when Collins took the stand. Here was the man who had seen everything that happened that fateful afternoon.

Collins began with the trip he had taken with his boss, Hubert Ward Jr., to the Ward property to pick up construction equipment. He told about Jerry Ward and Melinda coming out on the road and calling for help, about his going with Jerry's father across the road to Jerry's property, about the shoot-out with Jones and the boys, their surrender, the shooting of Larry Jones, and his tying the hands and feet of the three victims with wire. Finally, he gave the testimony that he had seen the boys alive for the last time as he drove the company truck out of the yard.

"Just before I pulled the truck out of the field to cross the road and load it up, I cut the headlamps on. The boys were in the field beside the fence where the chicken coops are, still on their knees at that time. Jerry Ward was standing a few feet away, holding a shotgun on them. There was a smaller figure behind Jerry."

Collins would be the last witness who saw the boys still alive late that night, apparently at the mercy of Jerry and whoever was standing behind him, presumably Melinda Ward.

But had someone else come to the farm later that night, Jake Nixon wondered. In his testimony, Collins had said Hubert Ward Jr. had said, "We have to wait for the big man." That left the unanswered question: What part did "the big man" play in the boys' execution? Had "the big man" participated in the execution, or merely given the orders to kill the boys? And the biggest question of all who was this mysterious "big man"? He seemed to lurk like a dark, shadowy specter behind the horrible, tragic murders.

Collins's testimony under questioning by the district attorney took up the remainder of that afternoon and was resumed the next morning.

Finally, Collins was turned over to the defense attorney for cross-examination.

Jake knew that Howard Collins was going to have a rough time in the cross-examination. Taylor had to discredit the testimony of Howard Collins or his client, Jerry Ward, was going to spend the rest of his life in prison. Jake felt sure that Taylor would pounce on Collins' plea bargaining and try to convince the jury that Collins would say anything the State told him to say in order to save himself.

Taylor: "Now, Mr. Collins, what did you do last night after you testified?"

Collins: "I went back to jail."

Taylor: "Did you meet with General Thompson last night?"

Collins: "Yes, I did."

Taylor: "And did he tell you what kind of questions I was going to ask you today?"

Collins: "He told me what you would probably speak on the most."

Later on, Taylor asked, "How much time did you spend with him Sunday night?"

Collins: "I do not recall. Hour maybe."

Taylor: "Hour. What were you all talking about then?"

Collins: "We were going over the case." Taylor: "Going over what he was going to ask you?"

Collins: "My statement."

Taylor: "And going over your testimony, weren't you?"

Collins: "Yes, sir."

Taylor: "And going over what he was going to ask you and what you were going to answer, weren't you?"

Collins: "He was giving me a general idea of what I would be facing."

Taylor: "What were you and General Thompson doing when you all were together Saturday?"

Collins: "We were discussing my statement, going over it."

Taylor: "What night did he get with you and take you up to your lawyer's office up in Lafayette and talk to you? That was one night last week, wasn't it?"

Collins: "Yes it was."

Taylor: "Okay. And the night before that you met with him, too, didn't you?"

Collins: "Possibly. I don't remember: I had met with him on several occasions."

Taylor: "Yes, you had. You met with him about ten or twelve nights in a row, didn't you? How much time have you spent with him, Mr. Collins? How many different occasions since you made this deal with him? How many times have you been with him?"

Collins: "I would say roughly ten hours." Taylor: "How many times have you been in this courtroom, Mr. Collins?"

Collins: "This is the third time."

Taylor: "When was the first time?"

Collins: "Right after I was arrested."

Taylor: "Hadn't General Thompson brought you up here and walked you through the courtroom and showed you where you was going to sit and where the jury was going to be and where I was going to stand and where the judge was going to be and all that?"

Collins: "Yes, he did. This is the fourth time." Jake Nixon

could see why Eddie Taylor was considered to be a topflight defense attorney. He was out to show the jury that Howard Collins had been carefully instructed and coached by the prosecutor.

Taylor then hammered away at Collins about his plea bargain deal.

Taylor: "Well, you cut your deal back in April, didn't you? You went up and you plea-bargained back in April. Don't you remember?"

Collins: "That's correct."

Taylor: "And you all had been working on that deal for a month or so before that, hadn't you?"

Collins: "My lawyer, I suppose, had."

Taylor: "And you originally was offered ten years, weren't you?"

Collins: "From my understanding from my lawyer, yes, that's correct."

Taylor: "But you wouldn't take that, would you?"

Collins: "No, sir."

Taylor: "And you all sort of dickered and sort of dealt back and forth, sort of bargained like buying a car or something. Because they wanted you to testify, didn't they?"

Collins: "My attorney did."

Taylor: "Uh-huh. And they wanted your testimony, didn't they?"

Collins: "Obviously."

Taylor: "And you knew that when you were bargaining with them, didn't you?"

Collins: "Yes, sir."

Taylor: "And did your lawyer also tell you that this accessory after the fact is not even an included offense of first degree murder, second degree murder, or any of those?"

Collins: "I wasn't aware of that."

Taylor: "But you all were trying to get something that you could come in here and show this jury though, weren't you? Something to get you up here, but something to get you out of here pretty soon after this trial is over, weren't you? That was your idea, wasn't it?"

Collins: "My idea was to get out of jail and get out of this mess the best way possible I could."

Taylor: "Right. That's one thing we agree on, Mr. Collins. Now, as part of your deal, you went into jail here in September, didn't you?"

Collins: "Yes, sir."

Taylor: "And when you cut your deal for six years, as General Thompson said, that was for thirty percent, wasn't it?"

Collins: "That's correct."

Taylor: "And you know how much thirty percent of six years is, don't you?"

Collins: "Roughly fourteen and a half months."

Taylor: "And tell us when you're going to get out of jail, Mr. Collins?"

Collins: "I don't know."

Taylor: "You're telling this jury that you haven't looked on a calendar to see when you get out of jail?"

Collins: "No, I haven't."

Taylor: "You know you're going to be home by Christmas, don't you? You're expecting to get out of jail at the end of November, aren't you?"

Collins: "I'm hoping, but I'm not expecting it."

Taylor: "You know you've got to do fourteen months or a little more before you're eligible for release, is that right?"

Collins: "That's correct."

Taylor: "And you know that fourteen months is in November, don't you?"

Collins: "Roughly, yes."

At one point in the cross-examination, the defense attorney tried to discredit Howard Collins's statement that during the shoot-out, Jerry Ward had a .32 pistol. The autopsy found .32 bullets in the victims. The gun that fired those shots had never been located.

Collins made the statement, "As Jerry walked behind me, I asked him, 'What have you got in the pouch, money?' He said, 'No, I have a .32 pistol. I've been waiting seven nights, been laying out here seven nights, waiting for these people to show up.'"

Taylor tried to make the point that Collins had made a number of statements to the law officials over the period of time since he had been arrested and there were some discrepancies between the statements. Collins defended himself, saying that he had time to remember more details as he reflected on the events. Taylor implied in his questioning that Collins wanted to cooperate with the district attorney and say what was necessary to strengthen the State's case in order to lighten his own sentence.

In the end, Jake Nixon doubted that the defense had made much of a dent in Howard Collins's testimony. Jake was impressed with Eddie Taylor's skill as a courtroom attorney, but Collins had told a simple, straightforward, convincing story of what he had seen that day of the fatal shooting. It was hard not to believe him.

There was one exchange between Taylor and Collins that Jake found extremely interesting.

Taylor said, "Okay. Now, Mr. Collins, I believe you said, if I'm not mistaken-and if I am, you tell me-I believe you said

that Hubert Ward told Summers and Larry Eugene Jones that
he'd have to make a decision on what to do with them when
the big man got there. Is that right?"

"That's correct."

"And you don't know who that big man is, do you?"

"No, sir."

The "big man" again. Jake thought he could be the key to
unlock what really happened at the Ward farm the night the
boys were executed.

"Now, Mr. Collins, you also said that when you and Mr.
Hubert Ward were loading up this Jones truck, that you turned
the lights on and you saw Jerry Ward watching the two people
that hadn't been shot. And you saw someone else, didn't
you?"

"Yes, sir, I did."

Eddie Taylor made an attempt to plant in the jury's mind
that another person, possibly the "big man," might have
arrived and been on the scene as Collins was pulling out of the
yard in the company truck. Collins had said that he'd briefly
turned the headlights on and had seen the boys on their knees
with Jerry Ward and someone else guarding them. He implied
that he thought the other person was Melinda Ward because it
looked to him like a person with a small frame.

Melinda was somewhere around there while Collins was
pulling out of the yard. More than likely, she was the person
Collins saw near Jerry Ward and the boys. But he wasn't
certain. Suppose the big man they had talked about had
arrived? If it was a small-framed person, then "big" would
refer to his being someone in power, higher up, rather than his
physical description.

It was a tantalizing thought.

For the remainder of the second day and for the days

following, the prosecution brought a string of witnesses to the stand. There was Ricky Claridy, the tobacco cutter, who told of smelling marijuana on the Ward farm, and going there late one night with friends to steal a grass sack full of the top grade pot. He told of Jerry Ward, carrying a gun, visiting the tobacco cutters and telling them that someone was stealing his "chickens" and he was going to put a stop to it. There was no doubt in Claridy's mind that the "chickens" Ward was referring to was the marijuana.

There was Thomas East Scruggs and Melinda had gone to his house the day of the shooting, asking for help to fight off intruders who had invaded the Ward farm. He said he was so spaced-out from medication that he was unable to go with them, but he loaned them a shotgun. A few days later, he said he saw Jerry Ward and asked about the intruders. He said Jerry Ward told him, "They didn't get away."

The families of the victims were present in the courtroom throughout the trial. Polly Summers said, "We had to set there in the courtroom right behind the ones that they had accused of killing them. Can you imagine what it is like to set right behind somebody that you think rammed a shotgun in your child's mouth and shot him?

"It was terrible to go in the bathroom and see Melinda. We had to use the same bathroom. We had to go in the bathroom and see Melinda standin' there, laughin' and talkin' about it. One day in there she was laughin' and talkin' about some of the children in her family. Some kid in her family-about how pretty he was, talkin' about that little boy's eyes. And she said Jerry said his eyes were just like his, and I said, 'Do you remember Kenny's eyes? Kenny's eyes changed color depending on what mood he was in, but he ain't got no eyes no more.' I said, 'His whole head was shot off.' It didn't bother her a bit."

Hubert Ward III, known as "Little Hubert," took the stand.

Under questioning from the district attorney, he said that he lived in Nashville where he worked in the construction trade. He said that he had been drinking heavily at the V.F.W. hall the day of the shooting. Late that afternoon, he had received a phone call from his father, Hubert Ward Jr., telling him they were having trouble at the family farm and they needed for him to drive over there. He said that he had not seen much of Jerry in the past year, that there had been some kind of family disagreement. In spite of that; and as drunk as he was, he drove from his home in Nashville to the Ward farm, arriving after dark

Continuing his testimony, Hubert III said that his father told him some people had tried to take over the farm that afternoon. The Wards thought others might come before the night was over. Hubert III was told to stand guard. He said that he sat down and leaned against the garage wall. A shotgun was propped beside him. He said he then went to sleep sitting there. He awoke about two o'clock in the morning. "It was quiet. Very quiet." He got up and drove home to Nashville.

According to his testimony, he did not see any of the victims or hear any gunshots. He just got to the farm, spoke briefly with his father and Howard Collins, then sat down and went to sleep beside the garage.

When he was cross-examined, the defense attorney went into more detail about his drinking habits.

Eddie Taylor: "Now you said you'd been at the V.F.W., is that right? All day on the third, drinking?"

Hubert: "Yes, sir."

Q. "How much would you say you'd had to drink that day?"

A. "Probably twelve beers. And between a pint and a fifth of tequila."

Q. "Do you know what time you went out there?"

A. "About eleven-thirty or twelve noon. Something like that."

Q. "Okay. And you'd just been sitting out there, drinking all day?"

A. "Yeah."

Q. "When was the first time that you heard anything about possibly bodies being found on the Ward farm?"

A. "On the news. The evening news."

Q. "And that was on the day they were found?"

A. "Yes, sir."

Q. "Now, Mr. Ward, after you left Jerry's place there that night, did you do back up there between September 3 and September 17?"

A. "No, sir."

Q. "Did you call up there the next day to see what had happened?"

A. "No, sir."

Q. "Didn't have any contact with Jerry Lawrence from then on?"

A. "No."

Q. "You didn't see Jerry shoot anybody?"

A. "No."

Q. "Before September 3, how often would you go out to the v.F.W., drinking?"

A. "A couple of times a week"

Q. "And that couple of times a week, you would be drinking, is that right? Normally? Right?"

A. "Normally. Yeah."

Q. "Would you go there after work? Or how would you do it?"

A. "After work"

Q. "And how long would you normally stay?"

A. "Couple of hours. Sometimes more. Sometimes less."

Q. "Did you drink at home, too? Drink a few beers at home at night when you'd get in?"

A. "Sometimes."

Q. "You drank pretty much-a little beer on a daily basis?"

A. "I didn't miss many days." Q. "Do you drink now?"

A. "I stopped."

Q. "When did you stop?"

A. "September 4."

Q. "Why did you quit drinking on the fourth of September, Hubert?"

A. "Pretty good time to quit."

Q. "You don't drink any now?"

A. "Right."

Q. "Do you do things when you're drinking that you ought not do?"

A. "Probably."

Mr. Taylor: "That's all."

Later, Jake Nixon discussed the testimony of Hubert Ward III with his editor, Hal Bevans.

"Do you think he was telling the truth?" Jake's editor asked.

"Hard to say. Little Hubert is in a difficult spot. He waived immunity, so he could still be indicted. I think the most ' important bit of information that came out of his testimony is the fact that he quit drinking abruptly on September 4, the day after the shooting, and hasn't had a drink since. Here's a man who was a real heavy drinker-probably verging on alcoholism. It takes something pretty earthshaking to make an alcoholic go on the wagon that abruptly. If you ask me, he quit drinking because he's running scared-scared of something he might say or reveal if he gets liquored up and starts shooting off his mouth. What is he scared of? Did he see something he isn't telling? Did he see the boys executed? Did he take part in the execution? Or is it something else? Is he afraid of this 'big man' that keeps cropping up? Is there some kind of connection between the pot being grown on the Ward farm and the Mafia or some higher-up drug dealer? Is Little Hubert afraid of being the target of a professional hit man if he talks too much?"

"There is a contradiction in his actions," the editor agreed. "On the one hand, he says he didn't see anybody tied up on the farm that night, didn't see anybody shot. In fact, he didn't see anything. He just sat down beside the garage and went to sleep, got up about two in the morning and went home. He says he didn't have an inkling of the murders on the farm until two weeks later--on the seventeenth. Yet, he stopped drinking abruptly on the fourth. Doesn't quite add up, does it?"

The trial continued with the State bringing in a number of forensic experts from the Tennessee Bureau of Investigation. Among them was a ballistics expert who testified that one of the bullets taken from the heads of the two boys was from a .32 caliber weapon.

Next, from the coroner, came the chilling, detailed description of exactly how the boys were executed, the guns that were used, and how many times they were shot.

Chapter 15

Doctor Charles Warren Harlan, medical examiner, was the State's next witness. The district attorney began by establishing Doctor Harlan's credentials.

Doctor Harlan stated that he was a physician whose specialty was that of pathology, more specifically anatomic, clinical, and forensic pathology. He received a Bachelor of Science degree from the University of Tennessee in Knoxville. His Doctor of Medicine degree was from the University of Tennessee Medical School in Memphis, Tennessee. He stated that he was certified by the American Board of Pathology in the fields of anatomic, clinical, and forensic pathology.

Harlan stated that he was the medical examiner for Nashville, Davidson County, and the deputy chief medical examiner for the middle third of the State of Tennessee.

The district attorney asked, "In your work as a forensic pathologist, how many autopsies have you done in your career?"

Doctor Harlan answered, "Thousands."

"And have you testified in federal and state courts both?"

"Yes, sir."

"Do you have any idea how many times you've testified, Doctor Harlan?"

"In excess of 300 times."

"And have you been accepted in the past as an expert in this particular court?"

"Yes, sir."

"And other courts?"

"Yes, sir."

The district attorney, General Thompson, then addressed the bench. "Your Honor, at this time I'd move that Doctor

Harlan be accepted as 'an expert in forensic pathology."

The Court: "All right, General. As you've said, he has been so accepted."

The testimony then began with General Thompson questioning Doctor Harlan.

Q. "All right. Now, Doctor Harlan, let's get down to what we're here for. On September the 17, or 18, 1985, did you receive a request from Trousdale County, along with three bodies, with a request for autopsies, to try to determine the cause of death of these bodies?"

A. "Yes, sir. I did."

Q. "And do you recall the names of the three?"

A. "Yes, sir. I do."

Q. "What were their names?"

A. "They were subsequently identified by me as the bodies of Larry Gene Jones, Larry E. Jones, and Kenneth Summers."

Q. "All right. Now, let's first take your autopsy of Larry Gene Jones. Is that number OC85-60?"

A. "Yes, sir. It is."

Q. "And did you perform an autopsy on it?"

A. "Yes, sir."

Q. "What was the condition of the bodies you received, Doctor Harlan?"

A. "The condition of all three bodies that I received, including that of Larry Gene Jones, was that of each being a decomposed, well-developed, well-nourished white male. This particular individual was uncircumcised, and had a stated age of thirty-eight years."

Q. "And how did you identify him?"

A. "The body was identified on the basis of comparison of the remains that we had with the known height, weight, and hair color, with the tattoos that were present, with the clothing that was present, and with dental work."

Q. "All right, sir. And was this body totally clean?"

A. "No, sir."

Q. "Describe what you found on the body."

A. "The remains that we received were clothed in a dark blue button-down shirt, old blue jeans. The body was caked in a gray-brown muddy material with straw, and there was some white caked material streaked through the gray, brown muddy material on all three bodies."

Q. "All right, sir. Now, on this particular body of Larry Gene Jones, were there any foreign matters attached, or connected to the body?"

A. "Yes, sir. There were multiple loops of silver wire, which were around both the left and right wrists, and the left and right ankles. There was also a loop of cloth that extended around the lower lip and the upper portion of the lower lip and the upper portion of the chin."

Q. "Was this loop of cloth loosely around him or tight?"

A. "It was moderately loosely around him, and it was reddish in nature."

Q. "Do you recall anything protruding out of his mouth?"

A. "No, sir. I do not."

Q. "All right, sir. Now, when you do an autopsy like this, what is the first thing that you do, Doctor Harlan?"

A. "The first thing we do is to identify the remains. Once that is done, then the wire is removed and is appropriately tagged. The gag or the material that was around the head in a loop fashion was removed, and the clothing was removed."

Q. "What did you do with the wire and clothing? What happened to that?"

A. "The wire that was removed, I tagged, and signed the tag stating where it was removed from, and signed that tag.

The clothing was removed by officers, I believe from Macon County, and was retained in their custody until they submitted it to the Tennessee Bureau of Investigation crime laboratory."

Q. "Did you give the wires to the Macon County authorities too?"

A. "Yes, I did."

Q. "Doctor Harlan, I hand you a group of six wires, State's exhibits 127A and B. Do you recognize those wires and the package attached to them?"

A. "Yes, sir. I do."

Q. "Are they the wires that you removed from the three bodies?"

A. "Yes, sir. They are."

Q. "Are the wires that you removed from Larry Jones there?" .

A. "Yes, sir. They are."

Q. "All right, sir. Are those the wires that you turned over to Deputy Ferguson to take to the crime lab?"

A. "Yes, sir. The two bags containing the wire from the body of Larry Gene Jones have been tagged as State's exhibit 129A and 129B."

Q. "When you received these bodies, did they have shoes, Doctor Harlan?"

A. "I don't believe so."

Q. "After you made the identification and after you removed the wires and tagged them, and after you got the clothes, did you do an examination to see if he had been injured?"

A. "Yes, sir. I did."

Q. "Is it difficult when a body is in that condition sometimes to tell exactly where all the injuries are?"

A. "Yes, sir. It is."

Q. "Did you make a determination as best as possible,

where he was injured, and what type injuries he had?"

A. "Yes, sir. This examination is a multipart examination. The first thing that is done is the body is X-rayed to determine the presence or absence of any projectile that might be present. We also examine for the presence or absence of certain other foreign material that might be present such as knife blades, et cetera. Once that is done, then the body is examined on external appearance for any possible gunshot wounds or shotgun wounds, stab wounds, et cetera. Then the body is charted-that is a notation will be made on a form showing where the different injuries are-then the body is autopsied, and all projectiles, knives, et cetera, that may be present in the body are recovered."

Q. "All right, sir." (State's exhibit 157 marked)

Q. "Doctor Harlan, I hand you what's identified as State's exhibit number 157. Who documented that sheet of paper?"

A. "The writing on this paper is mine."

Q. "All right, sir. And what is that, Doctor Harlan?"

A. "This is a copy of special chart 11 which is a portion of the autopsy report that we do, and this particular special chart 11 comes from the autopsy of Larry Gene Jones, with the autopsy number OC 85-60. OC standing for out of county autopsy, 1985, the sixtieth autopsy."

Q. "All right, sir. And you show a speckled area on his right side. What is that?"

A. "There's an area of the right side of the chest and abdomen which shows an area of shotgun pellet wounds. This area of shotgun pellet wounding extends from forty inches to fifty-seven inches above the heel, for a total space of seventeen inches."

Q. "Seventeen inches from the bottom shot to the top shot, is that what you're saying?"

A. "Yes, sir. That is correct."

Q. "And now, would you go further into your examination and tell us more about those shots and what damage was done?"

A. "Yes, sir. Examination of the body showed that the height of the individual was sixty-eight inches above the heel. The body had numerous tattoos, and these tattoos included a tattoo of the word 'Mickey,' spelled M-i-c-k-e-y, on the right shoulder. A tattoo of a dove on the right shoulder. A tattoo of a woman on the left breast, and a tattoo of the word 'Timmy,' spelled T-i-m-m-y, on the left shoulder. An Indian chief tattoo present on the left upper arm. A woman tattoo present on the lower left arm, a cross tattoo present on the back or dorsum, spelled d-o-r-s-u-m of the left lower arm, and the back of the left hand. And flower tattoos present on the back of the left hand. On the upper portion of the right forearm on the back was a tattoo, '**I** love you,' and on the back of the right hand there was a tattoo of a cross with the word 'Billie,' spelled B-i-l-l-i-e, inside the cross. The anterior or front lower right quadrant, or lower right portion of the abdomen showed a scar which was consistent with an appendectomy scar."

Q. "All right, sir. Now, what about the wound?"

A. "The shotgun pellet wounds that I previously described were present from forty to fifty-seven inches above the heel."

Q. "All right, sir. And what damage, or where did they go within his body? Could you determined where the shots traversed?"

A. "Yes, sir. I could."

Q. "Could you determine how many there were?"

A. "Roughly."

Q. "Roughly, how many?"

A. "There were approximately eighteen to twenty-five."

Q. "All right, sir. And tell us about where they traversed, and what organs they might or might not have hit."

A. "Yes, sir. The shotgun pellets entered the body and traversed the right lateral chest wall and abdominal wall with pellets striking the right lung, the diaphragm, and the liver. The pellets traveled from anterior to posterior, that is from front to back and from right to left."

Q. "Front to back and right to left?"

A. "Yes, sir. They passed diagonally through the body."

Q. "All right. Now, arid you told me about the damage to the organs, and did you determine the cause of death?"

A. "Yes, sir."

Q. "What was the cause of death?

A. "The cause of death was multiple shotgun pellet wounds to the right chest and abdomen, with the mechanism of death being bleeding and death from blood loss."

Q. "All right, sir. And where did this blood loss occur?"

A. "The blood loss occurred primarily into the right plural cavity."

Q. "Now ..."

A. "That's the right side of the chest."

Q. "And mostly on the inside of the body?"

A. "Yes, sir."

Q. "And, doctor, from a wound like that, do you have any opinion as to the time that it would take to bleed, based on that number of shots and the location where they hit, and the size?"

A. "Yes, sir. I do."

Q. "What would that be?"

A. "That it would take a fairly considerable period of time for the particular shotgun pellet wounds to cause death with death ensuing probably in one to two hours, perhaps a little less, perhaps a little bit more."

Q. "All right. Is there anything, Doctor Harlan, that I've left out?"

A. "Only the fact that I did recover multiple of the shotgun pellets and those pellets were in my custody until they were given to Chief Deputy Joe Ferguson of the Macon County sheriff's department at 1600 hours, which would be 4 o'clock p.m., on September 20, 1985."

Q. "All right, sir. And along those lines, did you send any tissue anywhere?"

A. "Yes, sir."

Q. "And who did you turn the tissue evidence over to?"

A. "The liver tissue was submitted to the TBI crime laboratory for analysis as far as the alcohol and drug levels and the results were provided to me."

Q. "All right, sir. You sent the tissue to them and they provide you the results and also provide us the results. Is that correct?"

A. "Yes, sir. That is correct."

Q. "All right. Now, let's move to the second body that you performed an autopsy on. That would be the body specifically of Larry Eugene 'Mickey' Jones. I don't know what order you took them in, but that's the order I'd like to take them in."

A. "Yes, sir."

Q. "Would that be OC 85-59?"

A. "Yes, sir."

Q. "Did you receive this body at the same time?"

A. "Yes, sir. I did."

Q. "And did you identify it?"

A. "Yes, sir."

Q. "How did you identify the body, Doctor Harlan?"

A. "The body was identified in going through the same

procedure that we went through on the body of Larry Gene Jones, and that procedure was to compare the height, weight, color of hair, and the fact that there were not tattoos present, the presence of a pierced left ear, which was present in the remains that we had, the known characteristics of Larry Eugene 'Mickey' Jones, the clothing which was present, and examination of the tissue."

Q. "All right, sir. What was the condition, and you don't have to be quite as descriptive, but was the condition of the body with regard to foreign matter the same as Larry Jones?"

A. "The remains of Larry Eugene 'Mickey' Jones were in approximately the same condition as those of Larry Gene Jones."

Q. "All right, sir. Did you find any foreign material attached to him?"

A. "Yes, sir. I did."

Q. "What did you find, Dr. Harlan?"

A. "There was loose gray wire which was around his hands or wrists, in front of the body, and wire wrapped around both ankles, with the wire around the hands and wrists being in front of the body as opposed to the wire of that of Larry Eugene Jones, that wire being wrapped around the wrists and tied in the back of the body."

Q. "All right, sir. And did you determine the age through the records, or so forth, of this particular body?"

A. "Yes, sir. The age was consistent with the stated age of seventeen years."

Q. "All right, sir. And did you find any other ligature ' items on him?"

A. "Yes, sir. I did."

Q. "What did you find, Dr. Harlan?"

A. "Examination of the body showed a loosely, tied loop

of coarse material extending around the neck. There were grooves on the side of the face which indicated that it probably originally was around and through the mouth area."

Q.'" All right, sir. Now, did-what was the condition of the head on that particular body?"

A. "The condition of the head was that there was some degree of disruption of the tissues, but not as severe as the disruption of the tissues of Kenneth Summers. The X-ray examination of the body showed the presence of numerous shotgun pellets in the head and the presence of a bullet which was recovered from the posterior aspect or the back of the left neck."

Q. "For the benefit of the jury, show where you're talking about. Point to it yourself, if you would, where the bullet ended up."

A. "The bullet was recovered in this area, and I'm pointing to this area of my body."

Q. "All right, sir."

A. "The shotgun pellets were recovered in two main groups on each side of the head, on the inside."

Q. "Now, do you have-did you X-ray the head, Doctor Harlan?"

A. "Yes, I did."

Q. "Do you have a copy of the X-ray?"

A. "Yes, I do."

Q. "Would you pull one, please?"

A. "Yes, sir."

Q. "Looking at that X-ray and you said the shotgun pellets were in two different areas. What would that indicate to you based on your expertise, Doctor Harlan?"

A. "The presence of the two groupings of shotgun pellets would indicate that two different shotgun cartridges were discharged or were fired with the pellets accumulating in one area here and the other set of pellets in an area here. This shows the presence of the bullet in this area. This is an anterior posterior, that means front to back orientation, and so the bullet in the neck appears in this location."

Q. "All right, sir. Looking at your X-rays, could you determine anything significant with regard to the bone structure of the head and face?"

A. "Yes, sir."

Q. "What would that be, Doctor Harlan?"

A. "There is fragmentation of the bony structure of the head to include the areas around the orbit or where the eyes would be to include the skull, which is fractured into numerous pieces, and to include the mandible or jawbone, which is fractured."

Q. "Did you make any determination with regard to the mandible or jawbone area?"

A. "Yes, sir."

Q. "Do you have any opinion with regard to that?"

A. "Yes, sir. That area was fractured by the explosion that occurred there."

Q. "All right, sir. Now is it your testimony that the entire bony area of the head was in pretty much disrepair?"

A. "Yes, sir."

Q. "Now, would you look at the face area and determine where the entrance of any bullet or shotgun blasts was from your physical examination?"

A. "Examination of the soft tissue and the bone at the mandible indicates that a gunshot is present in the point of the mandible or the jaw which is probably the point of entry of the bullet."

Q. "All right, sir. And that would be the bullet that wound up in the back, is that correct? In the back of the neck?"

A. "Yes, sir."

Q. "Could you tell where the shotgun wounds entered at all? Was there any way you could tell?"

A. "The shotgun pellets entered the body in probably two different locations."

Q. "Where would they be, Doctor Harlan?"

A. "They would have been such that one area would have gone to the right side and one area would have gone to the left side of the head."

Q. "Of the head. From the front or from the rear entrance?"

A. "The body was in such shape that I couldn't determine that precisely."

Q. "Doctor Harlan, based on your examination of this particular body, did you determine the cause of death?"

A. "Yes, sir. I did."

Q. "What would that be?"

A. "Death occurred as result of shotgun wounds ...and a gunshot wound to the head."

Q. "Doctor, based on your experience, you're saying that in your opinion there are at least two shotguns, that there are two shotgun blasts to the head or shots to the head?"

A. "The autopsy findings are consistent with two shotgun wounds to the head."

Q. "All right, sir. And they're also consistent with one pistol wound to the head. Is that correct?"

A. "They're consisted with one gunshot wound to the head."

Q. "All right. Gunshot. Excuse me. Gunshot. Based on what you saw and your examination, would you say any of these shots would be fatal?"

A. "Yes, sir."

Q. "Alone?"

A. "Yes, sir."

Q. "All right. One other question. With regard to the pellets and the gunshot bullet, what did you do with them, Doctor Harlan?"

A. "The pellets and the bullets were tested in a fashion similar to the pellets recovered from the body of Larry Gene Jones and they were retained in my custody and placed in appropriate containers until they were picked up by Chief Deputy Joe Ferguson of the Macon County sheriff's department at 1600 hours or 4 o'clock p.m., on September 20, 1985."

Q." All right, sir. And what about the foreign material, the wire that you described earlier, what did you do with it?"

A. "The wires and the clothing and the ligature were also given to Deputy Joe Ferguson."

Q. "Do you recall the color of that ligature that was around his head?"

A. "The ligature was an off color of pale material. Probably gray, yellow beige, white, something in that vicinity."

Q. "Now, the third body, which was-If

A. "Excuse me. The two ligatures contained relating to Larry Eugene (Mickey) Jones are labeled 128A and 128B."

Q. "And they are the wire ligatures that you turned over to Chief Deputy Joe Ferguson?"

A. "Yes, sir. They are."

Q. "And when you removed these wire ligatures, were they still in place doing the job that-were the hands still wired together and the legs still wired together when you removed them?"

A. "Yes, sir. They were."

Q. "All right. Now, let's look at OC 85-61, which would be Kenneth Lee Summers and pull your records on that one please, sir."

A. "All right."

Q. "How did you identify that body?"

A. "The identification on the remains received at the same time that two previous human remains were received was based upon a comparison of dental records, the color the hair, the absence of tattoos, the clothing that he was wearing which consisted of blue jeans and a white shirt with alternating light blue and dark blue and orange strips and an appendectomy scar which was present to the right lower quadrant of the abdomen."

Q. "Did you determine who it was and his age?"

A. "Yes, sir. The body was consistent with that of Kenneth L. Summers, a white male of the stated age of seventeen years."

Q. "And what was the condition of that body, Dr. Harlan, when you received it?"

A. "The condition of the body of Kenneth Lee Summers was consistent with that previously described of the other two human remains."

Q. "All right; sir. Would you describe whether or not there were any foreign ligatures attached to that particular body?"

A. "I did not observe the presence of any cloth ligature around the mouth area. There were wire ligatures which were present around the wrists and ankles. These wire ligatures being present with the hands or wrists tied behind the back and the wrists tied together with the ankles being tied together. "

Q. "All right, sir. And did you remove those ligatures?"

A. "Yes, I did."

Q. "And I ask you to look at the two plastic bags and give me the numbers of those, if you would."

A. "The two areas of wire ligatures were removed, the ligature from the wrists being labeled 127Band the ligature from the ankles being labeled 127A."

Q. "And what did you do with those when you removed them?"

A. "They also were given by me to Chief Deputy Ferguson of the Macon County sheriff's department."

Q. "Now, a description-would you give the jury some description of what the head was like on this particular body when you received it?"

A. "Yes, sir. There was marked disintegration and dismemberment of the head and face with the X-rays showing the presence of multiple shotgun pellets in the head area. The top half of the calvarius or the skull was absent and there were multiple shotgun pellets as well as two plastic shot casings recovered in the head. There were also two bullets which were present in the posterior portion of the head in the brain tissue. Two bullets were recovered and one was labeled OC 85-61Aand the other bullet was labeled OC 85-61B."

Q. "Did you keep them in your custody along with the pellets until you turned them over to some agency?"

A. "Yes, sir."

Q. "Who did you turn them over to?"

A. "Those pellets and shot casings and bullets were properly labeled and placed in manila envelopes and given by me to Chief Deputy Joe Ferguson of the Macon County sheriff's department again at 1600 hours on September 20th, 1985."

Q. "All right. So would you refer to your X-rays of the head of this particular body?"

A. "Yes, sir."

Q. "All right, sir. I'd like that marked for identification, also." (State's exhibit marked)

Q. "All right. Doctor Harlan, did you see the presence of the pellets that you are talking about?"

A. "Yes, sir."

Q. "Sir?"

A. "The X-ray shows the extensive disruption of the skull, the bones of the face including the orbit, the area of the nose, the mouth, et cetera. The X-ray shows that a portion of the maxilla with three teeth is located up here ..."

Q. "Where should it be, Doctor Harlan?"

A. "It should be down here."

Q. "All right, sir."

A. "The examination also shows the presence of multiple shotgun pellets and two bullets which are present in the area to which I'm pointing."

Q. "All right, sir. Can you look at that X-ray and point out the area where the two shot waddings are found?"

A. "No, sir. They do not appear on the X-ray because they are plastic and do not appear on X-rays."

Q. "That's right. It takes metal or something like that to appear on X-rays?"

A. "Yes, sir. Or bone."

Q. "Now, would you point to the area where they were found, or do you recall where they were found?"

A. "The bullets were recovered in the tissue in the back portion in what was left of the brain."

Q. "You say what was left of the brain. What do you mean by that?"

Mr. Taylor: "Your Honor, I object to that. That's inflammatory, prejudicial, and ..."

General Thompson: "I'll withdraw."

The Court: "Thank you, General."

Q. "What was the-compare the face, say of Larry Jones, that apparently didn't have any gunshot wounds to it. What was the condition of his face?"

Mr. Taylor: "I object to that also, Your Honor. That has no probative value." The Court: "I think it does. Go ahead, Doctor."

A. "The condition of the face was that the face was disrupted."

Q. "And when you say the skull and all is disrupted, what do you mean? And the face also?"

A. "I mean that it is blown apart."

Q. "Now, the same question I asked you a while ago. Based on your experience over the years, and looking at each of the wounds, would anyone of those apparent four gunshot wounds have been a death resulting wound?"

A. "Yes, sir."

Q. "Did you notice anything unusual about the- what is the area called behind the teeth, on the upper side, Doctor Harlan?"

A. "The maxilla, or the hard palate area, showed areas of defect. That is, there were circular areas of defect."

Q. "And they're in the back part of the mouth?"

A. "Yes, sir."

Q. "What about the teeth?"

A. "The mandible, that is the jaw, was intact. The maxilla was broken in two pieces with one piece which had the three teeth that I previously described as having been displayed upward, are present and separated from the rest of the mandible. There was also a tooth that was knocked out by the fracturing process which we recovered."

Q. "All right, sir. Did you determine the point of entry of any of these shotgun wounds?"

A. "The defects in the posterior hard pallet or the maxilla are consistent with points of entry."

Q. "Whether it be shotgun or pistol?"

A. "Yes, sir."

Q. "And that's in the back of the mouth?"

A. "Yes, sir."

Q. "Doctor Harlan, I hand you another drawing similar to the first two and ask you, can you identify that?"

A. "Yes sir, I can."

Q. "Is the writing on that yours?"

A. "Yes, it is."

Q. "And what is that?"

A. "This is special chart 11, more specifically, this special chart 11 is from the autopsy protocol OC85-61 of the autopsy of the body of Kenneth Lee Summers."

Q. "And the darker part on the left figure, the top of the head, what is that?"

A. "That shows the area of shotgun wound defect and the tissue being lost."

Q. "Doctor Harlan, I think you've already testified that you collected the wires and shotgun pellets and the gunshot bullets and turned them over to Joe Ferguson?"

A. "Yes, I did."

Q. "Did you do the same thing with regard to the body tissue?"

A. "Yes, sir, I did. The blood and bile samples were submitted to the Tennessee Bureau of Investigation crime laboratory"

Q. "Did you also turn over what items of cloth or clothing and turned them over to the authorities?"

A. "Yes, sir. I did. And those materials were also given to Chief Deputy Ferguson."

Q. "To go to the crime lab?"

A. "Yes, sir."

Q. "What did you determine to be the cause of death to Kenneth Summers?"

A. "The death of Mr. Summers occurred as a result of shotgun wounds to the head and gunshot wounds to the head."

Q. "And Larry Gene Jones, it's your testimony that he could have lived for an hour or two. What about these two young boys?"

A. "Death was essentially instantaneous."

Q. "Thank you, Doctor. That's all."

Mr. Taylor: "Doctor Harlan, in regard to Larry Eugene 'Mickey' Jones and Kenneth Summers, do you know what time of day they died?"

A. "No sir. I do not."

Q. "Do you know on what date?"

A. "No, sir. I do not."

Q. "You don't know whether they died on September the third or September the fourth or September the fifth?"

A. "That is correct."

Q. "Now, it is true, I believe from your testimony, that both Larry Eugene 'Mickey' Jones and Kenneth Summers were shot at least with two different weapons, is that right?"

A. "Yes, sir."

Q. "But you don't know who the person was who shot these people, do you?"

A. "No, sir. I do not."

Q. "Larry Gene Jones, I believe you said, bled to death?"

A. "Yes, sir."

Q. "That's internal bleeding?"

A. "Yes, sir."

Mr. Taylor: "That's all." General Thompson: "Doctor

Harlan. I just have one other question on the two different weapons. Are you speaking of the difference between a shotgun and a pistol? Is that what you mean by two weapons?"

Mr. Taylor: "Your Honor, I'd object to that. He hasn't said that the .32 was a pistol."

General Thompson: "Well, obviously one weapon would have been what?"

A. "One of the weapons that was used was a shotgun."

Q. "And the other was what?"

A. "The other weapon was a gun, be it a rifle, pistol, or revolver. "

Q. "That carries one single missile, rather than a group of missiles like a shotgun?"

A. "Normally."

Q. "Thank you."

The Court: "Thank you, Doctor Harlan. You may come down." (Witness is excused)

Later, Jake Nixon and his editor, Hal Bevans, discussed the medical examiner's testimony.

"That was some emotional dynamite," Jake said. "I sat there finding it hard to believe my own ears. Mickey Jones executed with a pistol shot and two shotgun blasts to the head. Kenny Summers, shot in the head twice with a .32, shotgun rammed in his mouth and the top of his head blown off. Then, as if that wasn't enough, a second shotgun blast to what was left of his head. My God, what kind of monsters would resort to that kind of carnage? It was bad enough to cold-bloodedly execute two seventeen-year old boys down on their knees with their hands and feet tied. That was cowardly enough. But to shoot them repeatedly!" Jake shook his head. "It was almost as if the murderer was in some kind of killing frenzy."

"Murderer or murderers," Hal Bevans, said. "It almost

sounds to me as if more than one person did the shooting. Does it seem possible that one person would shoot the boys with one weapon, then go pick up a different weapon and shoot them again?"

"That's quite possible," Jake agreed. "Two murderers could have been standing there, one with a .32 gun of some kind, probably a pistol, the other with a shotgun. They both start firing into the heads of the boys."

"The other possibility, I suppose," said Bevans, "is that there was a single killer. He shot the two boys in the head with his pistol, then, to make sure they were finished off, blasted their heads to pieces with the shotgun."

"But why shoot Kenny in the head twice with a shotgun? From what the medical examiner said, the shotgun was rammed in Kenny's mouth, knocking out some teeth. That blast blew the top of his head off. Surely there was no reason to blast what was left of his head with a second round from the shotgun."

"Doesn't make much sense," the editor agreed. "But a lot of things about this case just don't add up."

"My feeling exactly. I was hoping this trial would answer a lot of questions. At this point, it seems to me it has aroused more questions than it has answered. For example, Howard Collins testified that he tied the hands of both boys behind them. But when the bodies were found, Mickey's hands were tied in front of him. It would appear that after Collins left the scene, for some reason, Mickey's hands were untied, then tied again in front of him. Why?"

"Yes, and Doctor Harlan said there were no shoes on the bodies. Now, why and for what reason would the Wards remove the victims' shoes?"

Jake said, "Something the defense attorney said in his cross-examination brought up a possibility I hadn't considered. He asked Doctor Harlan if he could tell the time of death. In other words, could he be certain the boys were executed on the night of the shoot-out? The doctor said there was no way to be sure about that. The defense attorney went on to say that they could have been killed that night or the next day or even several days later."

"That's another baffling possibility," Hal Bevans agreed.

"But let's go on the assumption that they were killed on September 3, the night of the shoot-out. That's the most logical possibility. If Collins is telling the truth, after he and Hubert Jr. drove off in the truck that night, there were three people left on the Ward farm guarding the boys-Jerry Ward, Melinda Ward, and Hubert Ward III. The one thing about Hubert Ward III that bothers me is the abrupt way he quit drinking after the killing. He hasn't taken a drink since. He must have seen something or done something that night that threw one hell of a scare into him."

Jake agreed, "I've thought about that a lot. On the one hand, he says he and Jerry were not close and he hadn't been to the Ward farm much the past year. He talked about some kind of family difference. On the other hand, his father told the boys that they had to wait for the 'big man' to come to decide what to do. Little Hubert is anything but little. He's a real big man. Collins said he looked like a bear that night. It was established in cross-examination that Little Hubert didn't leave the Ward farm until two in the morning. A lot could have happened from the time Collins and the elder Ward drove off and two o'clock the next morning."

"There's also that possibility we keep talking about, that the 'big man' was some kind of higher-up drug dealer or organized crime figure or even a political person being paid off."

Both men fell silent for a few minutes, struggling with the complexities and contradictions of this puzzling case. Then Jake said, "There's one thing I can't get out of my mind. It will probably haunt me for years. Can you begin to imagine the terror and mental suffering one of those boys felt when he saw his cousin's head being blown apart and knew his turn was next?" .

The State concluded its case. The defense was brief, consisting mostly of bringing character witnesses who testified that Jerry Ward was a responsible citizen who had never been in any trouble with the law.

Then the prosecutors and defense attorney gave their final arguments. Both prosecutors, the assistant district attorney, John Wooten, and the district attorney, Tom P. Thompson spoke. They tried to convince the jury that they had proven their case, that Jerry Ward had been growing marijuana on his farm and because of that, the killings had occurred. Whether or not he was the one who pulled the trigger of the guns that killed the boys, he was clearly an accomplice and therefore, under Tennessee law, guilty of accessory to murder, a first degree crime.

The defense attorney, Eddie Taylor, argued that the State had not proven beyond a reasonable doubt that Jerry Ward had killed anybody and therefore should be found not guilty. In his closing statement, Taylor suggested that the killer could have been Hubert III or even Thomas East. He reminded the jury that East had been a lifelong friend of Jerry Ward, that he had supplied Ward with guns. He suggested that although East did not return to the Ward farm with Scruggs and Melinda when they got the shotgun from him, he might have gone to the farm later that night and could have been the triggerman.

The case went to the six-man, six-woman jury on Thursday

afternoon, May 8. They deliberated for two and a half hours. On Friday, the jury deliberated until 4:30 in the afternoon when they brought in their verdict.

Jerry Ward was found guilty on two counts of aiding and abetting the first degree murder of Larry Eugene (Mickey) Jones, seventeen, and his cousin, Kenneth Summers, seventeen.

The *Lebanon Democrat* newspaper described the scene in the courtroom when the verdict was delivered:

"Tension ran high in the courtroom Friday afternoon as members of the victim's family filled the seats directly behind members of the Ward family. Extra security measures were taken to ensure no 'emotional breakouts' occurred, Judge Bradshaw said.

"After jurors handed down the verdict, 'Guilty of Aiding and Abetting Murder,' nothing but silence could be heard throughout the smoke-filled courtroom. Ward sat stonefaced during the proceedings and in a rare moment throughout the week, spoke quietly to his father.

"As the verdict was read, Ward's sister, mother and wife quietly cried.

"'It's a tragedy,' Taylor said briefly after the verdict was given. 'The Wards have always been a nice family. I don't know what happened, but I think wrong was done.'

"Thompson and Wooten agreed, however, that the verdict was just. 'It was Jerry's marijuana that caused every bit of this,' Thompson said.

"Although no one but Melinda and Jerry Ward apparently know who pulled the triggers that killed the teens, where the executions occurred or when, Thompson last week theorized that perhaps the youths, whose hands, wrists and ankles were bound with wire, were put into the barn's grave, then shot repeatedly. Prosecutors said the case is rare because, as defense attorney Taylor repeatedly maintained, no one admits to killing the two boys or to seeing the act, and the murder weapons have not been found."

Less than two hours after delivering the verdict, the jury dropped a bombshell that stunned the community and sent shock waves throughout the legal system.

That evening, after going home, some of the jurors watched the six o'clock television newscast about the trial and verdict. The newscast anchorperson explained that the conviction of aiding and abetting a murder carried the same sentence as actually committing the murder. Each conviction carried a mandatory life sentence with earliest possible parole after eighteen years in prison.

The jurors said they were horrified. They had received detailed instructions from the judge. In spite of that, for some unexplainable reason, the jurors hadn't realized they were sending Jerry Ward to prison for life. They immediately contacted the defense attorney and judge and reversed their decision. A Macon County newspaper carried the following story:

"Criminal Court Judge Robert Bradshaw declared a mistrial in the week-long trial of Jerry Lawrence Ward on Saturday morning after members of the jury which convicted Ward told Judge Bradshaw they would not have returned such a verdict if they had realized the consequences of that verdict.

"Several jurors, one of them the foreman, said they first learned the verdict meant life imprisonment when they watched the six o'clock news about one hour after their decision to convict Ward was announced in a crowded Trousdale County courtroom.

"The jury foreman, Will Roddy, and a second juror, Kelly

Cox, went immediately to Ward's attorney, Eddie Taylor, and reportedly told him, 'There has been a mistake.'

"Taylor told reporters, 'The jurors said they didn't realize that aiding and abetting in a crime is considered the same for sentencing purposes as committing the crime itself.'

"The declaration of a mistrial in the case came after a series of meetings and calls that occurred between seven and nine p.m. Friday night between Ward's defense attorney, Eddie Taylor, prosecutors Tom P. Thompson and Johnny Wooten, and Judge Robert Bradshaw.

"Judge Bradshaw then called all twelve jurors before him Saturday morning and reportedly told them, It has come to my attention from several jurors, including the foreman first, that the jury would not have returned such a verdict if they had realized the consequences of that verdict.'

"The judge told a reporter that he asked for a show of hands from the jurors who felt that his information was accurate and all twelve of them-at least four of them in tears-raised their hands.

"'I believe they were sincere,' Bradshaw said. 'They simply didn't realize that an aider and abettor is punished as a principal offender, although the information was in the charge that I gave them to carry back to the jury room.'

"Judge Bradshaw said he 'felt compelled that my only choice was to declare a mistrial.'"

At ten o'clock that same morning, Jerry Ward was released from the cell where he had spent the night and went home.

The district attorney filed a motion for a new trial. The motion was granted and Jerry Ward was scheduled to be retried in November.

Chapter 16

EPILOGUE

This case has left many unanswered questions. I t has affected many lives. It has left puzzling mysteries in its wake.

For example, there is the mystery of Jerry Ward's brother, Bobby Ward is a member of the Ward family who has remained a shadowy figure in the background through all of these events. He is the one member of the Ward Family who did not attend Jerry's trial.

Shortly after Jerry's arrest, the Rinehart and Ward construction company fell on hard times and declared bankruptcy. Was it a strange coincidence? There is some speculation that the profits from the marijuana being cultivated on the Ward farm were funneled into the construction company. When the drug money stopped coming, the construction company failed.

There is the mystery of what happened to the prison record of Howard Collins.

Howard Collins seemed to vanish off the face of the earth after his parole. I did some detective work after the trial in attempt to clear up some of the unanswered questions in this strange case. I tried to track down Howard Collins to find out if he could shed any further light on this case.

In trying to locate what had become of Collins, I went first to the courthouse in Hartsville. I could find no Social Security number, no previous address, and no pre-parole interview. In the case of parole, Tennessee requires a pre-parole release. There is a requirement a parolees file are four immediate family who are always able to give the parolee's current address. None of that was in the court records at Hartsville.

I then went to the State Capital Building in Nashville to the Attorney General's Office. The secretary at the Attorney General's picked up the phone and made several calls, then handed me the phone. I then explained to the person on the other end of the line that I was trying to locate Howard Collins.

The woman on the phone asked me to spell Collin's name. Then she asked if I had a prison or file number on him. I told her that he might not have a file number because all of his time was served in a county jail, not in a state prison. She said that shouldn't make any difference. She told me that even though he served time in a county jail, they should have his case on record, but they simply did not have a data base file on him. She sounded a bit embarrassed..

I contacted the TBI Agent who had investigated the case. He was unable to locate Howard Collins. I hired a local Detective. He couldn't track down Howard Collins. I tried to find Collins through a Credit collection agency, but without a Social Security number that was a dead end. I had read in the trial transcript that Collins had been in the Pensacola Florida when the Ward family hired him.

As a last hope, I ran an ad in the Pensacola Paper. Success at last! Howard Collins answered the ad, calling me collect. I made a trip to Florida to interview him.

When I went to talk to him, he was terrified that I was there to harm him. He refused to go to to a hotel room. We couldn't find a suitable place inside the hotel, so we went out to the pool area.

I told him about the difficulty I'd had locating him; that I hadn't been able to find him in any court records. He said that he went to Florida after he got paroled from the Tennessee jail; When he contacted the local parole board , they said they had no record on him. He got in touch with Tennessee authorities and they had no record on him. He was having trouble doing his income tax, because he could not get any records from the Wards. He got in touch with the IRS and filed an estimated return for the last three years that he worked for the Ward Construction Company. At this time he had contacted the FBI. They ran a record check on him and said as far as they were were concerned, he had never been in Tennessee, had never been in jail, had no prison record, and was not on parole.

I asked him to go over his part in the events at the Ward farm on September 3. He told me exactly the same story he told in court. He repeated his statement, "At eleven o'clock that night the boys were still alive, Just before I pulled the truck out of the field across the road, I cut on the headlamps. They were in the field beside the fence where the chicken coops are, still on their knees at the time."

"It was very regrettable that I had to tie them up that way. I wish I'd never fired a gun. I wish I hadn't been such a coward to stand there and be made to tie them people up. They would still be alive today, if it hadn't been for me. My life is not worth living now, anyway. I was raised in a Baptist church. I can't understand why God allowed me to be involved in something like that".

"You see, after Larry Jones , the father of Mickey, was shot, I was scared to make any kind of move other than to just go along and hope to God they didn't turn on me. At one point I'm sure that they were discussing me also because they would go to the hill away from me and talk and they'd look over at me and go back to talking again.. They done that two or three times".

There is the nagging mystery of how Jerry Ward was able to negotiate the sale of a marijuana crop with an estimated street value of a million dollars.

I asked Collins is he had a theory about that. He said, "From sources, I understand that Thomas East was hauling the marijuana by boat down to Nashville where Hubert III was passing it on to different distributors".

It also aroused fresh questions of just how involved Thomas East and Hubert III were involved in this crime. In his summation the defense attorney had suggested that Thomas East or Hubert III could have pulled the triggers that executed the boys.

What really happened on the Ward farm on the night of September 3, 1985? The Wards said that they were waiting for "The big man" to decide what to do with the boys. Who was this mysterious "Big man"? That could be the biggest question of them all. If we find out who the big man is, it could re-open the case.

Eyewitnesses at Jerry Ward's trial who saw the lush, top grade marijuana crop before it was cut down estimated it's street value at a million dollars. In his trial testimony, Thomas East indicated that about one third of the crop was missing when Jerry was preparing to destroy the rest of the crop. What became of one third worth more than $300,000.00 ?

From trial testimony it is possible to reconstruct the events of September 3, 1985. Let us assume that Jerry Ward was raising the crop for someone else, "The big man", who was a big time drug dealer, powerful political individual, or organized crime figure. Jerry was getting only a pittance for his part in the operation. When Larry Jones and the two boys raided the farm the afternoon of September 3, Jerry Ward saw the opportunity to grab part of the crop for himself. After Jones ran Jerry away from the house, a half hour or more passed before Jerry ran out in the road calling for help. It would have been enough time for Jones and the two boys to have made off with some of the marijuana. Jerry could have then cut a large portion of the crop for himself; claiming the intruders had stolen it.

That plan failed when the Jones truck stalled. When the three became his captives, Jerry could still take part of the crop and blame it on the three if there were no living witnesses to say exactly what had been taken. He talked whoever was their into a death pact. Three people were involved. All three would fire shots into the boys at the same time. Nobody would know exactly who killed them, and who was shooting into a dead body, so nobody could tell on anyone else without convicting themselves. After the execution, Jerry harvested and moved the missing marijuana to another location. The killing of the two boys was not motivated by the desire for revenge or out of anger. It was to allow Jerry to steal almost one third of a million dollars from the higher up figure, his boss, and solve a bad situation at the same time.

I believe this is the true story of what happened on the Ward farm on September 3, 1985.

If this isn't what happened, then it is just another nice theory in a true crime puzzle that may never be solved.

The murder of Mickey Jones and Kenny Summers continue to affect many lives. Both families live with the grief on a daily basis.

Kenny's brother Wayne, is the member of the Summers family most seriously affected by Kenny's death. He suffered a nervous breakdown. He and his wife Debbie, divorced. He moved to another town. He did at one point, at the start, draw a map to the Ward farm and leave it with a deputy sheriff. Somehow the map disappeared. The deputy is now dead. Whatever the circumstances, it went to the grave with the deputy. He can't tell!

As for Melinda, Hubert Jr., and Jerry Ward, they got off with very light sentences considering the brutality of the execution of the two teenage boys.

Melinda Ward did not serve a day in prison. Before her trial date, the State of Tennessee agreed to a plea bargain. She plead guilty to cultivating marijuana. The state dropped all charges of accessory to murder. She received three years in prison, all three years were on probation. On New Years Eve, she became intoxicated and took out the city welcome sign at Hartsville. She made front page on that.

Hubert Ward Jr. also plea bargained his way out of a lengthy prison sentence. In his plea bargain, he plead guilty to one count of second degree murder and two counts of accessory to murder. His sentence was two years on the second degree murder charge and three years on each count of accessory to murder, for a total of eight years. Because of the overcrowding of the Tennessee prison system, only class X felons are admitted to the Tennessee prison system. Class X is rape, murder, or armed robbery. Anything else is served in local jails. Hubert Ward Jr. served his time in the Trousdale county jail, and some in the smith county jail at Carthage Tennessee.

Under those conditions, the person in jail never goes under the state parole authorities. The determination of time to spend in jail is made by the judge, who has the authority to release that person at any time. Hubert Ward Jr. was probated after serving approximately eighteen months in the county jails.

After Jerry Wards first trial was declared a mistrial by Judge Bradshaw, a second trial date was set for November of that year. Late October, the District Attorney, Tommy Thompson, arranged for a meeting with the families of Micky Jones and Kenny Summers. The meeting was held in Inez's home.

Thompson informed the families of the two slain boys, that he had been offered a plea bargain in the Jerry Ward case and he wanted to offer it to the families of the boys. Thompson made the statement that if the relatives agreed unanimously, he would abide by their decision. If there was no unanimous agreement, he would make the decision . Most, but most all of the twenty people assembled there were in favor of a new trial. Since there was not a unanimous agreement, Thompson said, "Based on my twenty years of courtroom experience, if we do try Jerry Ward a second time and don't get a conviction, when we go back to trial the third time, there is not a jury in this state that will convict him because each jury looks back to see what the preceding jury had done, and that influences their judgment.

Two days before Jerry's second trial was to begin, the families of Mickey Jones and Kenny Summers were informed that the district attorney had accepted a plea bargain. Jerry Ward would plead guilty to two counts of first degree murder, one count of raising and cultivating marijuana, and one count of accessory to second degree murder. The prison time was all bundled at twenty years. Under Tennessee law that meant that he would be eligible for parole in about one third of that time, approximately seven years. He entered the prison system early January 1987. In less than two years he had applied for parole. The first application was denied. In the following years he applied for parole, several parole hearings were granted, but parole was denied.

A lot has occurred since September 3, 1985, and today. Some things were truly remarkable! First, When Larry gene, Larry Eugene, and Kenny were listed nationwide as missing persons, Sherry, Larry Eugene's mother was never notified by any agency of the law. When the truck of Larry Gene's was found by the police; relatives, not police informed Sherry.

When the bodies were located, a news flash all, all but informed Sherry of the findings, and when positive identification was made, even though three different county sheriffs, State Police, TBI, Emergency Personnel, and the District Attorney's were all present; no one from that group of people notified Sherry that her son's body had been located and recovered. A family member bore that duty.

Almost every aspect of this case had some sort of unusual twist and turn. At the Ward's first trial, Inez, Larry Gene's mother , and the boys' grandmother said that she had seen the DA work much harder to send Larry Gene to prison for burglary, than he did at Jerry's murder trial.

After Jerry Wards short time served before he got his parole hearing; meaning that he could possibly be released on parole, the Parole Board was contacted with a letter and several names and addresses to be notified every time Jerry Ward was scheduled for a parole hearing . At the next parole hearing one of the eight names was notified, and of course that one notified the others.

Jerry's time in prison was just an inconvenience, not punishment or rehabilitation. He was assigned to serve his time in a minimum security prison, and accepted for work release. His family owned Charter Construction Company. That's who he worked for on work release. He would leave prison early in the morning, be bussed to his work site, and return at days end. During his sentence he got weekend furloughs, and left prison with the only requirement being , to be at the prison early Monday morning to go to his work place.

Sentenced to twenty years; fifteen years without a correction, a write up, or any type of prison violation, time was considered served since Tennessee law says 75% of time served with no problems is considered a serve out.

Questions about prison assignment, work release, levels of crime, time being served, was sent Tennessee Prison Authorities, with no reply.

Many of the people in this book have died. Below is the vitals listed on each person that could be located.

VITAL RECORDS SHOW;

NAME DATE OF BIRTH DATE OF DEATH

Hubert Ward II 9-15-1927 5-18-2007
Hubert Ward III 6-25-1971 11-4-2008
Charles Robinson 6-23-1929 3-7-2008
Inez Thaxton 6-14-1924 7-12-2007
Polly Summers 6-3-1940 4-22-2005
Billy Summers 11-10-2009 8-16-2009
Carl Summers 6-15-1962 6-9-2005

Melinda Ward There is no official record of death although her family says that she died from a cancerous tumor.

At last check, Thomas P. Thompson was still the DA. John wooten had become a judge in the area, but is still in the office with DA Thompson.

Reports of numerous cases with bizarre outcomes have occurred in the community.

In early 2010 Sherry was contacted about a possible film based on the book with a lead in, and expanded epilogue, to mark the 25th anniversary of the story.

These people came to our house in Kentucky. They come from Tennessee and disclosed their plan. When they learned Sherry had a transcript from the court reporter and that it was the one and only since the reporters house had burned , and all court related documents in her possession were destroyed; and the Wards trial transcript was among those, they borrowed our transcript ran copies, and returned the original in just a few days. They were to keep Sherry informed of their progress.

After several weeks she tried to contact them at their business phone; but it was no longer in service. Other attempts did not pay off. Finally, Sherry remembered the woman's name that came with them to get the transcript. After trials and failures, she was located. She told Sherry that she had been close friends with the two. Sally, the woman that Sherry was speaking to, told her that her partner had been working on something, and on the next Monday he planned to present it to the FBI.

At the end of the week, some time during the night, they cleaned out their office of anything considered to be of value, and their files. They left without a goodbye, disclosing a reason, providing a forwarding address, or leaving any information that would allow someone to contact them. She said Sally called once and told her that they were OK. She said that she would not tell where they were or what they were doing; only that she was in the gulf covering the oil spill.

What happened with these two people? What kind of danger were they in to cause them to "pull up and run"?

Just one more mystery in this story!

This story should be a wakeup call to the average American Family. With pot being the drug of choice today, there is probably no way an average family can keep their children away from this stuff. That being the case every parent needs to warn their children about how deadly people are at all levels of growing, manufacturing and selling this poison. Kids should know never, in any to trust, attempt to rip off, or try to steal from these people! They will kill you, regardless of age, sex, or religion. Even someone you may have known for a lifetime will kill you in a second, without thought or remorse, if you are any way a threat or danger to them.

Now as parents, you need to become involved and obtain some information for possible personal use.

You need to know how prison inmates are assigned to prison facilities. What criteria the prisoner must meet to become selected for work release. Is the level of crime (IE. Murder, rape, kidnapping, and armed robbery) used to determine which prison a prisoner is assigned to, and what programs he is eligible to receive. How much of a sentence must be served, and if any deals are available to shorten the sentence.

As parents you should know these things, just in case your child is charged and convicted of a crime, or is a crime's victim..

If you find similar faults in your situation, then please contact those people that can change the law. Then get your quest into the news, TV, radio, and newspapers. You will be surprised what public opinion can get done.

If you do not know your lawmakers, they are most likely listed in your phone directory, under government, or are available from your library, or community newspaper. Please do not put this off! Get started today!

If you think Tennessee law concerning sentencing, housing, furloughs, and work release needs to be changed; please write or call:

The Office of the Governor
State Capitol Building
600 Charlotte Avenue
Nashville TN. 37219
Phone(615)-741-2001

The DA's decision after Jerry Wards sentencing was, as

far as others that may be involved, "Isn't worth pursuing". This has allowed two killers to walk free all this time , and absolutely no one has ever or is now looking for them.

Many court procedures are based on prescience set by another earlier case, and the action of that court. When Judge Bradshaw ruled the mistrial for Jerry Ward, the verdict had been reached and delivered by the court. The jury had been polled to see if all agreed to the verdict, then dismissed. When Judge Bradshaw, Tommy Thompson, and Eddie Taylor agreed to reconvene court the next day; the judge said since the jury hadn't understood the consequences of their verdict, and he did not believe he could allow the jury to deliberate further, as they would be tainted from family, neighbor, and news media exposure. He said " I believe that we are breaking new legal ground here", meaning this was a precedence setting case, and could be used as reference if a similar situation arose; so a "mistrial" was declared.

How very strange that a decision in a tiny Tennessee Courtroom in an old weathered court house could have an impact in such a high profile and important trial's; such as Casey Anthony or Doctor Conrad Murrys'.

Even though the families of the victims feel that Jerry Ward pretty much escaped justice his life now is not so sweet. With the weight of the events that occurred on September 3rd, 1985 barring on his heart, mind and soul his mental stability has declined to the point he has few friends, and the ones he does have keeps a distance becouse they look at his as a timebomb capable of exploding at any time. It is reported that Jerry, has sence been released from prison, has been in atleast one mental institution and present day goes around talking to himself. It appears that the words in the bible are true, "vengence is mine" saith the Lord.